*Safeguarding a Truly Catholic
Vision of the World*

Safeguarding a Truly Catholic Vision of the World

Essays of A. J. Conyers

Edited by
Jacob Shatzer

With a Conclusion by
Bradley G. Green

RESOURCE *Publications* · Eugene, Oregon

SAFEGUARDING A TRULY CATHOLIC VISION OF THE WORLD
Essays of A. J. Conyers

Copyright © 2014 Jacob Shatzer. All rights reserved. Except for brief quotations in critical publications or reviews, no part of this book may be reproduced in any manner without prior written permission from the publisher. Write: Permissions, Wipf and Stock Publishers, 199 W. 8th Ave., Suite 3, Eugene, OR 97401.

Wipf & Stock
An Imprint of Wipf and Stock Publishers
199 W. 8th Ave., Suite 3
Eugene, OR 97401

www.wipfandstock.com

ISBN 13: 978-1-62032-880-4

Manufactured in the U.S.A.

Permissions from various publications acknowledged within text.

Contents

Introduction: Safeguarding a Truly Catholic Vision | vii

1. Teaching the Holocaust | 1
2. Protestant Principle, Catholic Substance | 16
3. Cloning and the Moral Imagination | 21
4. The Changing Face of Baptist Theology | 25
5. Three Sources for the Secular Mind | 47
6. Simms's *Sabbath Lyrics* and the Reclaiming of Sacred Time in Religious Imagination | 57
7. Vocation and the Liberal Arts | 72
8. As Bad as We Get | 85
9. Can Postmodernism Be Used as a Template for Christian Theology? | 91
10. The *Real* Old Time Religion | 111

Conclusion, by Bradley G. Green | 121

Bibliography | 125

Introduction
Safeguarding a Truly Catholic Vision

It is always interesting to look back at what shapes and guides a person's theological vision. In my first semester as an undergraduate at Union University, I took Old Testament Survey with Brad Green and fell in love with theology. In my second semester, I enrolled in Christian Doctrine with Brad, and found myself being guided by A. J. Conyers, a theologian few in our class had heard about. Conyers's *A Basic Christian Theology* served as our course text. While the book proved to be an excellent introduction to theology, it wasn't until my final semester—when I sat in Brad Green's office with one other student for our Theology Seminar—that I can say I really fell in love with the work of Conyers. In that class we read his newly published *The Listening Heart*, a work that put Conyers's depth of knowledge and keenness of insight on clear display. In my doctoral program at Marquette University, I found myself consistently returning to Conyers, and I decided to write a dissertation on his work. My theological vision and voice will always bear its mark.

I am not entirely sure what attracted me so strongly to Conyers. Part of it was his clear writing and sharp insight, but I think more than that I was attracted by the vision of the world that Conyers had. Between my first exposure to Conyers in the spring of 2004 and my first reading of *The Listening Heart* in the spring of 2007, Conyers tragically lost his long battle with cancer and passed away. His grand vision of theology and ethics, rooted in the Bible and shaped by the Great Tradition of Christian theology, emerged clearly in his final books, but as I continued to dig up articles that he wrote, I found new and surprising treasures. It is my desire to share these pieces

Introduction

with a wider audience that I have collected several of the most important into this volume.

Abda Johnson ("Chip") Conyers III was born May 29, 1944.[1] He spent his formative high school years in rural Georgia and showed an early interest in American history, especially Southern history and culture. He studied at Young Harris College, where he met his wife, Debby. The two married in 1964, and Chip attended the University of Georgia with plans to pursue a career in public service or law. He taught school for a year after graduating from Georgia, and during this time he began to sense that God had a different call on his life, a call to ministry. He earned the MDiv from Southeastern Baptist Theological Seminary, and the PhD at the Southern Baptist Theological Seminary. He graduated in 1979 after writing a dissertation on Jürgen Moltmann under Dale Moody. Chip and Debby even spent six months in Germany for research. Moltmann continued to hold something of a spell over Chip, as even Chip's latest work shows engagement with new works by Moltmann.

Yet Chip was not simply a Moltmannian. (His critical reception of Moltmann is a story for another book.) Another major influence on Chip was an older form of conservative political thought, espoused by the likes of Richard Weaver. Chip molded these two sources of inspiration and formation—Moltmann and conservatism (and others, of course)—into a unique perspective for a theological engagement with the modern world.

The essays that I have collected here demonstrate a few characteristics of Conyers's work. First, the breadth. In these pieces he deals with wide-ranging issues, from the Holocaust to cloning to liberal arts to theological method to internecine Baptist theological issues. And that doesn't even include his philosophical acumen or his theologically driven literary criticism or his work on Protestant-Catholic thought or his reflections on speciesism and even Islamic fundamentalism. Second, the depth. Conyers shows an ability to ascertain the heart of an issue and then deal with the heart in depth. Third, the creativity. Conyers constantly made connections between issues, demonstrating in his very analysis the interconnectedness of biblical studies, historical theology, systematic theology, ethics, and church life.

I am sure that I seem to err on the side of hagiography and fanboyism. I certainly do not want to communicate that Conyers finally found the perfect theology, or that he never made mistakes. (For one, I think he flirted with Social Trinitarianism, which lurks in at least one of these essays.) But

---

1. This biographical information can be found in Conyers and Conyers, "Biography."

Introduction

I do not hesitate to insist that Chip Conyers had a lot worth saying. He saw the world in ways that few do, and he was quite good at describing his view. He took to calling it a "truly catholic vision of the world," not to take anything away from Roman Catholics, but to insist that there was something abiding, something worth recovering, that lies back behind that Catholic-Protestant split. Chip wanted to safeguard and promote that vision of human flourishing.

Though Chip is no longer with us, his writings still are, and they continue to ring with truth and insight. I hope that this collection will draw more people to his work, to his "truly catholic" view of the world, and ultimately to his commitment to the kingdom of God.

1

Teaching the Holocaust

The Role of Theology (1981)[1]

NOT A FEW PROFESSIONAL and learned societies are looking into the topic "Teaching the Holocaust" in hopes of introducing the study of this twentieth century experience to secondary and college classrooms. What they are discovering should be of no small consequence to theologians: namely, that theology has an indispensable role to play in the adequate treatment of such studies. It makes an arresting discovery indeed if we consider that the chief impetus has come from the faculties of state universities and public school systems, and not generally from theological faculties. As momentum is gained, and more avenues come to light, it has occurred not only to theologians, but to others as well, that the subject matter almost compels us to raise questions that are more akin to theology than any other discipline. This means that now, while great interest is shown in the public sector of education, where history and other liberal arts subjects are often treated to almost fastidious secularity, one is faced with the task of teaching that which seems to call urgently upon a theological response.

In this paper, therefore, I simply want to underline and reinforce this initial intuition on the part of educators: that the Holocaust cannot be taught adequately without reference, at some point, to the theological questions it raises. That is to say, any attempt to do so without a theological point of reference leaves interpreters to deal with what is nothing less than a historical "black hole" in the midst of Western civilization. It is not

---

1. Originally published in *Perspectives in Religious Studies* (1981): 128–42.

that theologians have answers that ring with clarity and assurance while all the rest struggle. Quite the contrary: these problems should bring the theologian as much anguish as anyone. It is precisely because the Holocaust strikes at the roots of *his* confession, and calls into question the validity of *his* discipline, that he is called into the arena. And furthermore, that responsibility devolves upon him not because it is his private province, but because the questions are broadly human questions for which he has taken some responsibility.

Why is this so characteristic of the Holocaust? It is no accident that the Holocaust of the 1930's and 1940's has become the topic of wide ranging theological discussion in the 1970's and 1980's. The Holocaust is not the kind of event that one might elect to view theologically, along with other options. It is *essentially* a theological problem. This is true for at least two reasons:

1. To put it most simply, *the Holocaust is different from most other calamities and human disasters in history*. True, life has been counted cheap before: more have lost their lives in a shorter period of time; the weight of monstrous crimes has fallen upon specific ethnic or religious groups and even upon the Jews before; in all of remembered history, in fact, the scales of justice are never balanced and the blood never ceases to flow. However, what we deal with here is different in two specific ways:

    a. *It is different from the standpoint of the oppressors*, because here is the story not simply of men presuming to take the lives of others for, say, temporal gain, or out of passion. But here are men, acting in Promethean defiance against the given order of reality, to violently reshape history itself: to bring in a new order—a millenium—a Thousand Year Reich. In order to achieve this transcendent goal, some at least, are willing to make human sacrifice.

    b. *It is different from the standpoint of the oppressed*. Here, after all, is an event that, for many Jews, could and did call into question their covenant relationship with God.

2. Additionally, *the Holocaust raises, in the most dramatic way, the problem of evil*: the origin of evil, the persistence of evil, evil and human nature, evil and the nature and/or existence of God. Even if it is negatively stated (e.g. Wiesel's "Never shall I forget those moments which

murdered my God and my soul and turned my dreams to dust"[2]), the events inevitably raise questions about the relationship between pervasive, planned, and prolonged evil and the transcendent meaning of our existence that includes such evil. This sort of question is inevitably part of the Holocaust experience, and to deal with it at any level is to resort to theological categories.

Even as we advance the reasons for looking at the Holocaust as a theological problem, I think that we are already suggesting the two areas in which theology might be the greatest help. The first has to do with the problem of *man and evil*: how could twentieth-century man so easily have surrendered to his darkest impulses? Why should this have happened in the context of what we had come to believe (and not without justification) was the apex of civilization—not only in the twentieth century, but in twentieth-century Europe? The other line of questioning has to do with the problem of God and evil—theodicy: how is it that such evil as one encounters in the Holocaust exists at all? We are faced with the dilemma, in the words of Archibald MacLeish, "If God is God he is not good; if God is good he is not God." We will attempt now to indicate some helpful directions that have been taken in theology, beginning with these two problems. In the first instance Richard Rubenstein, a Jewish theologian, and Helmut Thielicke, a Christian theologian, provide arguments upon which to focus. With regard to the second problem, attention is given to Jürgen Moltmann, a Christian theologian whose insights in this area owe much to Abraham Heschel, the Jewish theologian.

The Holocaust and the Problem of Evil in Human History

The penultimate problem of the Holocaust comes to one's attention first. The ultimate problem is a problem of theodicy, of justifying God or of understanding existence itself in the light of stultifying evil. But before that we must face the less comprehensive, but no less necessary, question of the nature of humanity as this concept is affected by the possibilities for human evil that were revealed at Auschwitz and Treblinka.

One approach has been to place these events within the context of certain historical forces and attempt to understand, in terms of social and political theory, how these events might have come about. The question

---

2. Wiesel, *Night*, 44.

that emerges runs like this: How does it happen that ideological excesses in the twentieth century, not altogether different from those found in earlier centuries but which were then confined to fringe elements, suddenly erupted into huge mass movements capturing reputedly civilized nations? What defenses against these ideological excesses are missing in the twentieth century that have opened the flood gates, as Rubenstein has pointed out, on a century of mass death—a phenomenon by no means confined to Germany of the Third Reich? "We are more likely to understand the Holocaust," Rubenstein says, "if we regard it as the expression of some of the most profound tendencies of Western civilization in the twentieth century."[3]

The most characteristic feature of Rubenstein's attempt at a theoretical basis for the Holocaust is that he refuses to see these events, monstrous though they be, as isolated in history, wholly attributable to the Germans, and divorced from other peoples and movements in the twentieth century. Instead he presses his investigation to discover the similarities in thinking which made possible the mass deaths directed by the American use of the atomic bomb in Japan, and associated with the administration of British colonial rule, as well as with the Bolshevik revolution and its consequent intensification of terror and mass death. These and many other instances suggest to him a certain pattern of events in our century apart from which the Holocaust cannot adequately be considered.

If one refuses to isolate the Holocaust from its historical context, and from the broader context of Western culture, he immediately is faced with a complex web of events and attitudes which present themselves as possible contributors. Rubenstein focuses basically upon three developments of greatest significance, as he believes, in understanding the Holocaust. The first relates to the way modern nations have faced and dealt with their population problems. For at least three centuries Europe exported its surplus population to North and South America. By the beginning of the twentieth century the American frontier had closed; possibilities for solving population problems in this way diminished. At the same time the twentieth century witnessed untold slaughter in World War I, the loss of hundreds of thousands of young men who were considered expendable for the sake of the goals of war. The problems of population became acute after World War I when the drawing of new national boundaries and the relocation of whole nationalities resulted in a critical disordering of communities. The *apatrides*

---

3. Rubenstein, *Cunning of History*, 21.

or stateless persons naturally presented difficulties in overcrowding; but the difficulties in view here are not simply that. There is also a perceived population difficulty that might be described as a certain demographic untidiness that is presented by groups, within a national population, that are not wholly or easily or satisfactorily absorbed into the prevailing ethnic group.

Rubenstein asks, in effect, if the occurrences of mass deaths, up to and including Holocaust, might be more than coincidentally related to the twentieth century's population crises. "Is it not possible," he asks, referring to the slaughter of British and German troops in World War I, "that some automatic, self-regulating mechanism in European society was blindly but purposefully experimenting by means of war with alternative means of population reduction?"[4] He notes that population control mechanisms come into play among overpopulated animal species. Could it then be that the unparalleled death march in the twentieth century is really in response to historical forces that act with a cunning indirectness? Rubenstein leaves us with little more than a provocative question at this point. But here he ties in two other points that relate to the Holocaust phenomenon.

One is the institution of slavery, an institution that survived to its latest forms in the Americas. The importance of slavery in this discussion is that it depended, to a degree, upon considering a human being as an instrument, dominated in whole, or in large part, by his owner. Rubenstein notes Cotton Mather's reference to slaves as "the Animate, Separate, Active Instruments of other men."[5] Especially in industrialized societies, slavery became largely an inefficient means of production. What Marx described, and Rubenstein thinks not altogether inaccurately, as "wage slavery" was a more efficient means of dominating human beings for the larger purposes of society. But the issue in either case is that the efficiency of the slave system depends upon the degree to which the slave can be treated as a thing rather than as a person. It depends upon the depersonalization of the slave. The more complex the economy, or the more it moves from an agrarian to an industrial economy, the greater the demand for efficiency. Slavery in both North and South America only imperfectly anticipated the slavery of death camps in twentieth century industrialized Europe; and that imperfectly, writes Rubenstein, "because of their failure to eliminate all human involvement between the rulers and the ruled."[6]

4. Ibid., 10.
5. Quoted in ibid., 3
6. Ibid., 36.

Safeguarding a Truly Catholic Vision of the World

However, the earlier institutions of slavery can be seen as links in a process that moved toward an increasingly rationalized system of domination. While American slavery was less than the completely rationalized system of near total domination found in Nazi death camps, it represents a higher degree of domination than earlier instances of slavery. Those conditions which allowed the Nazi camps to secure such domination is expressed by Rubenstein in this way:

> Slavery in North America was thus an imperfectly rationalized institution of nearly total denomination under conditions of a *shortage of productive labor*. The death camp was a fully rationalized institution of total domination under conditions of a *population surplus*.[7]

It was this surplus population, made so by definition, and condemned to death, that made the institution of slavery in the camps one that responded to the demands for efficiency in a highly complex economy. The full efficiency required of this slave society could be reached because, in this case, the condemned status of the prisoners made it all the more possible to relate to them as things rather than as human beings. The death camps played a part that Rubenstein thinks is often overlooked. They were not simply the means of carrying out a genocidal policy and thus satisfying ideological demands. The camps were, more significantly, a new form of society—a society of total domination in which the inmates could be treated as completely expendable and thus as mere "separate, animate, instruments."

These ideas of domination, efficiency, and depersonalization find their center in Rubenstein's discussion of the development of bureaucracy. While slavery in North and South America never reached levels of total domination, the death camps of Germany did so to a remarkable extent. The mechanism that made this possible, Rubenstein explains, was the highly developed German bureaucracy, a bureaucracy whose greatest achievement was to work within society in a detached and impersonal manner. Rubenstein proposes that a certain barrier to the resolution of population problems was transcended by the possibilities that lay at hand in a bureaucratic system. While the "obvious" solution was deterred by religious and moral restraints, a well-developed bureaucracy offers a means of minimizing those restraints.

---

7. Ibid., 41.

This is precisely so, Rubenstein argues, because the highest virtue of bureaucracy is that it can respond in a highly rational and impersonal manner. While everyone within the bureaucratic system responds to a given situation, in the course of bureaucratic action, no one is altogether responsible: thus situations are met not by a person, but by the faceless system itself. To support his point, Rubenstein calls upon Max Weber who was well aware of bureaucracy's significance in this regard, however innocent he may have been of its ultimate application. Weber notes:

> When fully developed, bureaucracy stands . . . under the principle of *sine ira ac [sic] studio* (without scorn and bias). *Its specific nature which is welcomed by capitalism develops the more perfectly the more bureaucracy is "dehumanized,"* the more completely it succeeds in eliminating from official business love, hatred, and all purely personal, irrational and emotional elements which escape calculation. *This is the specific nature of bureaucracy and it is appraised as its special virtue.*[8]

One might be convinced, therefore, that bureaucracy is not disuaded by the most ghastly program: it performs the task it is designed for, no matter how morally reprehensible, *sine ira et studio*.

A cultural undercurrent, essentially religious, has made the development of such a bureaucracy possible, explains Rubenstein. "Bureaucracy," he said, "can be understood as a structural and organizational expression of the related processes of *secularization, disenchantment of the world*, and *rationalization*."[9] The roots of this disenchantment are in the theology of Israel. The whole of creation is placed over against its Creator as the source of its existence. Therefore, in Israel's understanding of God's relationship to the world there is no room for independent powers within creation: all divinity is apart from and above the world. In the Christian doctrine of the incarnation we see an "attempt to find once again an intrinsic link between the supramundane realm of divinity and the desacralized human order which had become devoid of magic or mysterious forces."[10] And in certain aspects of Roman Catholicism there is an attempt to re-enchant the world. Protestantism, however, represents a violent rejection of this attempt, and marks a decided shift toward an emphasis upon the transcendence of God and his "utter withdrawal" from the created order.

8. Quoted in ibid., 22. The emphases belong to Rubenstein.
9. Ibid., 27–28.
10. Ibid., 29.

Without in any way laying the blame for the Holocaust on Protestantism, Rubenstein does point out that the land of the Reformation "was also the land where bureaucracy was able to create its most thoroughly secularized, rationalized, and dehumanized 'achievement,' the death camp."[11] The special danger of the disenchantment of the world, an important element in Jewish and Christian theology, is the depersonalization of the world order. The special danger of depersonalizing and objectifying the world order is the depersonalizing of humanity itself, and of man's relationship to man. The greatest expression of this danger is seen in the fact that it was not the fever pitch of the German SA early in Hitler's Reich that posed the greatest danger for European Jews, but it was the bureaucratic calculations of Himmler's SS, and the terrifying simplicity and thoroughness with which the bureaucracies of Europe became unresisting instruments of a genocidal ideology.

It is quite clear in Rubenstein's treatment that bureaucracies are peculiarly suited to such tasks as the Nazi ideology assigned them. And it is evident that only in a fully dehumanized system can death be indiscriminately administered to Jews, Poles, Gypsies, the mentally ill, and others, whom the German hierarchy had delegated to the level of *Tiermenchen* or subhuman beings. Even as he argues his point, however, it seems that he shows it is not entirely adequate to speak only of bureaucracies, their theological bases, and of a tradition of slave domination. These are structural considerations; and however important they are, it seems that more must be said about basic personal attitudes and convictions. Rubenstein hints at this when he points out that the bureaucratic administration of the death camps was most efficient and dispassionate when *human* relationships between the camp officials and inmates were kept at a minimum. Measures were taken, for instance, to prevent the SS from developing personal relationships with female prisoners. "At Auschwitz," Rubenstein notes, "several brothels were organized in order to minimize the temptation to resort to unauthorized liaisons."[12] By making this point, of course, he is implying that it is not bureaucracy pure and simple that enables the task of enslaving and killing to be carried out efficiently; but that very efficiency must be supported in other ways and particularly by maintaining the fiction that the victims are not human. As long as they remained emaciated and wretched, and as long as personal relationships were not allowed to develop, it became all

---

11. Ibid.
12. Ibid., 44.

the more possible to consider these victims as *Tiermenchen*, and thus more bearable to impose torture and extermination.

By his own explanation of the system, it seems that Rubenstein invites a look beyond the dehumanized bureaucracy and into the mind that fails to perceive humanity. It is not a bureaucracy that, in the final analysis, defines certain groups as subhuman. The bureaucracy may respond to such an ideology, and may be well suited to administer its program, but what is at issue here is a fundamental view of man. While Rubenstein deals with a great part of the problem in a helpful manner, it appears that he does not adequately treat that which ultimately decides whether or not a bureaucracy can respond to ideological demands such as the National Socialists placed on it: namely, how human beings are determined to be expendable.

At the beginning of this section, we raised the question of why the twentieth century appears vulnerable to ideological excesses that have been current, though kept ineffectual, for several centuries. Rubenstein helps to answer that question by saying, essentially, that now the instruments and traditions are at hand to be used in the service of any ideology that gains the ascendancy, and in response to the need for population control. We also need to see, however, what it is that allows an ideology to gain such stature in a reasonably civilized and humane community.

This further aspect of the matter is treated with particular clarity by the German theologian Helmut Thielicke, and it bears directly upon the question at hand: man's capacity for evil. Thielicke was one whose early and sustained resistance against Nazism caused him later to reflect upon why his resistance and that of others like him was of such little effect and why, indeed, it failed to stop what all around them sensed in the "beating wings of darkness" that which, when fully revealed, could only be described as Holocaust.[13] He attempts to answer this question by dealing at length with a number of pragmatic barriers. Then he writes:

> But despite all the important factors which I have mentioned I should be passing over the most important reason of all for this guilt and catastrophe if I did not make the following statement: It is my firm conviction that the ultimate reason why all this could have happened is theological in nature.[14]

---

13. Thielicke, *Between Heaven and Earth*, 146–59.
14. Ibid., 159.

What he speaks of is "two extremely different views of man." One view sees man in terms of functional worth. He is the bearer of erotic attractiveness or of biological value (such as in the doctrine of a master race), or he is raw material in the historical process (as a member of the proletarian class). "And inherent in this concept," says Thielicke, "is the . . . consequence that 'worthless life,' like a machine which no longer functions, must be scrapped. In this case the term used is liquidate."[15]

The opposite view of man involves what Luther called an "alien dignity" which means that man's worth is entirely apart from his immanent functional value. His value rests upon the fact, as Thielicke puts it, "that God loves him, that he was dearly purchased, that Christ died for him, and that therefore he stands under the protection of God's eternal goodness."[16] It was the absence of such a concept of man, Thielicke concludes, that left the German people practically defenseless against an ideology whose logical conclusion was genocide. People could recoil in horror years later and say "no, but we never meant that!"—but they had failed to recognize that same evil when it was only provocative talk in the Munich beer halls.

The fact of the Nazi death camps is a witness to the loss of this fundamental understanding of human dignity and its source. Thielicke explains this point in a discussion of torture in his first volume of *Theological Ethics*. Torture, he says, bypasses man's humanity: it does not seek decision so much as it seeks response; the humanity is reduced to the instrument of another's will. Thus the "infinite worth of the human soul" (von Harnack) is replaced by a worth in terms of what the market will bring, and there is consequent readiness to violate and even liquidate the person for the sake of certain specified ends.[17]

Thielicke makes the compelling argument, therefore, that the one concept that resists such violations of human dignity is that which removes the source of man's worth entirely away from his usefulness (to himself or to others or to society) and from any phenomenological considerations whether they be race, economic class, political loyalties, mental health, or any other. Rather it has strictly to do with a relationship, one that is revealed in the conviction that the person is an object of God's love—a love that is inexplicable and utterly apart from man's immanent utility.

---

15. Ibid., 160.
16. Ibid., 163–64.
17. Thielicke, *Theological Ethics*, 646.

As Thielicke discusses this concept of "alien dignity" it is partially based upon Luther's doctrine of justification, the principle thesis of which is that man is "sinful in fact, righteous in hope" (*peccator in re, justus in spe*). It is not man's present condition that defines his relatedness to God, but that which God alone can know and make real. Therefore his worth cannot be based upon his immanent value either to himself or others, for its realization is effected only by the loving faithfulness of God. Thielicke (following Luther at this point) treats the doctrine of *imago dei* within the framework of justification, making clear that, *at no point*, is man's worth that which he bears independently, but it is something that can neither be possessed by one man, nor taken by another. Thielicke writes:

> The divine likeness is thus, in the first place, that which man *in re* no longer is, but on the basis of which he is nonetheless addressed. It is that lost state in which he was when he first received his being from the hands of God, and which he cannot escape—inasmuch as he is constantly being addressed on the basis of it—though it is in the negative mode that he must necessarily live it out.
>
> However, the divine likeness is, in the second place, that which is to be received afresh in Christ as a quality *in spe*. It is thus something which is given to man, and has to be given again. Consequently, it expresses not man's own immanent and ontic dignity, but that alien dignity which is grounded in and by him who does the giving.[18]

In Thielicke's analysis one sees that the theological response can be taken a bit beyond Rubenstein's. It is not enough to say that a tradition of domination, perfected by bureaucracy, that is in turn underpinned by a disenchanting theology led to the Holocaust. It must also become clear why individual and collective conscience was so ineffective against these events. A bureaucracy may become quite impersonal, and apparently very machine-like in its operation, but it never operates without people and without communicating ideas and attitudes that must be understood and cannot help but be evaluated. It is the nature and deficiencies of that communication among people in Germany (be they officers in a bureaucracy or not) that Thielicke finds important. To the extent that there were dangerous failures to apply critical judgment, he finds that the cause was a loss of conviction concerning the nature and worth of man: a misplacement, in effect, of the locus of man's value as man. The result was not directly the

---

18. Ibid., 169–70.

Holocaust, since we could easily see those same attitudes present in other parts of the world where such tragedies have not occurred. The effect was a certain vulnerability—and an inability to resist the genocidal ideology of Hitler at a moment of national crisis.

The Holocaust and the Problem of Evil in God's Economy

Over a decade ago Rubenstein also dealt with what we are calling the ultimate question that the Holocaust presents—namely, the theodicy question—in his book *After Auschwitz: Radical Theology and Contemporary Judaism*. In this collection of critical essays he made the point that most Jewish theology since World War II had ignored the enormous fact of the Holocaust and its inevitable effect upon Jewish life and thought; and that once this earthquake within the life of the community is adequately considered, the only satisfactory choice for theology would be to affirm the statement, made during those days by Altizer, Hamilton, and others, that "we live in a time of the death of God."[19] Now that we live "after Auschwitz" he saw no other alternative. William Hamilton, he said, was the first to suggest that he, Rubenstein, should be included in the ranks of the death of God theologians. Rubenstein first declined the designation, then agreed to it:

> After reflection, I concluded that Professor Hamilton was correct. There is a definite style in religious thought which can be designated death-of-God theology. I have struggled to escape the term. I have been embarrassed by it. I realize its inadequacy and its Christian origin. I have, nevertheless, concluded that it is inescapable. I see no other way of expressing the void which confronts man where once God stood.[20]

It soon becomes clear, however, that Rubenstein's difficulty with conceiving of God in view of the Holocaust rests upon the idea of a God who remains aloof from the suffering, who could effect a change if he would, but who

---

19. Rubenstein, *After Auschwitz*, 151. He maintains, further, that such devastation as the Jewish community has endured is bound to have radical results in its life and thought: "I believe the greatest single challenge to modern Judaism arises out of the question of God and the death camps. I am amazed at the silence of contemporary Jewish theologians on this most crucial and agonizing of all Jewish issues. How can Jews believe in an omnipotent, beneficent God after Auschwitz? . . . No man knows the hour when the full impact of Auschwitz will be felt, but no religious community can endure so hideous a wounding without undergoing vast inner disorders" (153).

20. Ibid., 152.

refuses. "I do not believe that a theistic God is necessary for Jewish religious life," he says.[21] Judaism, as a tradition and inheritance through which experiences are shared, remains, even though "we no longer believe in the God who has the power to annul the tragic necessities of existence."[22]

All of this, it would seem, leaves an opening to new developments in Rubenstein's thinking. It is not clear from *The Cunning of History* how much Rubenstein's earlier radical theology might have changed, if at all. What is clear in the earlier book, however, is that, for Rubenstein, theology "after Auschwitz" rejects only a certain idea of God. By the death of God he means "the demise of the God who was the ultimate actor in history."[23] The question could be well placed here: What if that God were also the sufferer and the servant, and not only Lord omnipotent? The question is perhaps not one to put to Rubenstein; but it is one for which Rubenstein leaves an opening when he calls into question a God who is the God of history—the Deuteronomist's God who is responsible for all things, and ultimately for Auschwitz itself. What he calls for is a redefining of the role of God, and although his own attempt may be rejected, it invites theological inquiry at a very basic level. Drawing from the vocabulary of the mystics, he says, "I am willing to believe in God the Holy Nothingness who is our source and our final destiny, but never again in a God of history."[24] Such a redefining has met with little acceptance either in the Jewish or Christian theological communities. But the problem continues to be posed: how does one conceive of God in view of the enormity of mass death in our century?

Ironically, at about the same time Rubenstein was rejecting the "God of history" concept on the basis of Auschwitz and the theodicy question, others—notably certain eschatological theologians—were finding that the evils of the Holocaust, and the theodicy question generally, *required* a God of history. One of the most imaginative and sustained efforts to deal with the theodicy question in the light of these events comes from one of the most prominent of these eschatological theologians, Jürgen Moltmann. Basically he would maintain that the Holocaust has caused us to reexamine any view of God as an impassive transcendent reality and to think—along with the biblical accounts—of a God who suffers. That is to say that one response to the question of suffering and evil consists not in justifying a God

21. Ibid., 153.
22. Ibid., 154.
23. Ibid.
24. Ibid., 204.

Safeguarding a Truly Catholic Vision of the World

who is untouched by pain, want, temptation, and evil: but in a view of God who responds to suffering by taking it on himself. He is not a God of apathy (no suffering) but the God of pathos who moves man to sympathy (suffering with). With this Moltmann returns to the insights of Rabbi Abraham Heschel who in his Berlin dissertation of 1936 and in his book *The Prophets* called the theology of the prophets a theology of pathos.[25]

In contrast to Rubenstein, it is precisely in the concept of a God of history, a God who enters history not immediately as Lord but as vulnerable fellow sufferer and servant, that Moltmann addresses the theodicy problem. In that God has a history, he suffers the risks, uncertainties, and dangers of history. In Christian theology particularly, he experiences the godforsakeness and existential alienation that man suffers in history. In a word, it is in the history of God, joined as it is to the history of man's redemption, that we see why the incarnation is nothing less than a response to the problem of theodicy. Unfortunately, Moltmann makes his point concerning God as a God of history at the expense of theism, an element in his thought that I would argue (although not here) is not self-evidently necessary.[26] Nevertheless he makes this one point clear: the center of Christian theology—and less explicitly, but nevertheless in reality, of Jewish theology—is the incarnation of God.[27] It is that which makes it possible to say that the suffering of man is taken up in the suffering of God.

Pursuing this thought Moltmann calls to mind a tragic tale from Wiesel's *Night*. In the concentration camp at Buna a child was condemned to be hanged along with two men. Prisoners were compelled to watch the execution. The men died quickly. The boy writhed in torture for a long time. "Then someone behind me asked: 'Where is God?'" "No one answered. After half an hour he cried out again: "Where is God? Where is he?' And a voice within me answered: 'Where is God? . . . He hangs there from the gallows.'"[28]

Moltmann recognized the importance of an incarnational theology when he said:

---

25. See Moltmann, *Crucified God*, 270–72.

26. Ibid., 249–52.

27. In his views on the coincidence of Christian and Jewish theology, Moltmann is influenced by Rosenzweig's *Star of Redemption*. See Moltmann, *Church in the Power of the Spirit*, 136–50, under "The Church and Israel."

28. Wiesel, *Night*, 70–73. Retold in Moltmann's *Experiment Hope*, 73.

A theology after Auschwitz would be impossible, were not the *sch'ma Israel and* the Lord's prayer prayed in Auschwitz itself, were not God himself in Auschwitz, suffering with the martyred and the murdered. . . . The God of action and success would let us forget the dead which we still cannot forget. God as Nothingness would make the entire world into a cosmic death-camp.[29]

The god incarnate cries to us from the pain of the cross, from the depths of Auschwitz, not alone from the throne of heaven.

This brief focus is only a beginning.[30] But it is perhaps enough to demonstrate the necessity of theological reflection in this area of study. Rubenstein, Thielicke, and Moltmann have followed a line of inquiry that others are now finding a compelling one. It is not to be wondered then, that educators find cause to turn to theology in this urgent task of remembering the Holocaust and interpreting it for a generation far removed—and yet too near to forget.

---

29. Moltmann, *Experiment Hope*, 73.

30. Other basic resources in a theological understanding of the Holocaust and of ideological mass movements in the twentieth century include: Arendt, *Origins of Totalitarianism*; Ellul, *New Demons*; Niemeyer, *Between Nothingness and Paradise*; Fleisher, ed., *Auschwitz*; Berkovitz, *Faith after the Holocaust*.

2

Protestant Principle, Catholic Substance (1996)[1]

THE INTRAMURAL DIALOGUE OVER what Mark Noll has called "the scandal of the evangelical mind" worries that intellectually serious people have passed evangelicals by while we were allured by the sensations of revivalism, seduced by a materialistic market-driven culture, overtaken by the "disaster of fundamentalism" in the face of challenges from modern science and technology, and robbed of our universities through negligence and the inertia of secularized education. At last we have lost the thread of an intellectual tradition that leads all the way back to the Reformation itself—a Reformation led, as Jaroslav Pelikan once reminded us, by a "cadre of intellectuals." The discussion stalls, at this point, for want of a painfully obvious question—an outsider's question really, but one that we evangelicals ought to consider if only for the purpose of dismissing it: Is there something in Protestant thought itself that, doing the work of a computer virus, finally renders impotent even the best of the Protestant intellectual tradition?

For instance, the Protestant conviction that Scripture should be a more or less unmediated guide to the believer naturally raises objections to an academic theological guild, which smacks of intellectual elitism. The offense of academia sometimes lies in the fact that it bothers itself with small things. Scholars make distinctions where others do not see any distinctions. They show parallels that are not readily apparent, and become apparent to the larger populace only after a steady effort to make the thing known. Such

---

1. Originally published in *First Things* (November 1996): 15–17.

enterprises seem, at first blush, antithetical to the democratizing spirit of Protestant Christianity.

Specialists, however, serve others, not themselves. That is true in every field. Theology along with biblical studies is for everyone, but it is done well by those who have worked at it enough to make it their specialty. That doesn't mean that it is for the specialist, any more than Ford automobiles are for engineers, or that the Chrysler building is for architects. But it is a work done by a few in the Church for the sake of all—a perfectly sound New Testament concept, and in the end soundly democratic as well.

In *The Christian Intellectual,* Jaroslav Pelikan underscored this dilemma by saying that the most formidable obstacle to the renewal of Christian intellectual life is "a curious alliance between the secular suspicion of an elite that has been characteristic of much of American life and a distorted interpretation of the Reformation doctrine of the universal priesthood of all believers." Just as America symbolizes a repudiation of old European aristocracy, "so Protestantism is represented as a repudiation of the hierarchical structures and traditions of medieval Catholicism." The result, Pelikan wrote, is a leveling that "regards the emphasis on scholarly merit and intellectual competence as dangerous and that therefore prefers the schooling of the many to the educating of the few."

It is of course not true that small matters in every area of life have become intolerable to the populist tastes of evangelicals. It is specifically the "airy" quality of intellectual concepts that offend evangelicals, as well as most moderns. In the late middle ages, Western people began to lose confidence in universals. This is explained as the philosophical change from realism to nominalism, from a belief in universals as real to a belief in the fundamental reality of unrelated particulars. But it was more than a philosophical shift, reflecting the reliance upon *facts*, things that occur to the senses. Intelligible reality was thought more and more an expedient, an arbitrary classification of things that conveniently arranged and made sense of the facts. But what was *real* was the existence of sensible facts, and the intelligible things were mere categories and *names* of things.

With the emergence in the modern era of the natural sciences, learning as a whole became imitative of the natural sciences: and this is no wonder, since the natural sciences brought spectacular results. It was easy to believe that the method of these sciences was not merely successful in its own realm, but that it held the key to knowledge itself, to human learning of any kind. Science in this modern sense moves from concrete facts to theoretical principles. The latter are subject to change, and the former exact from modern science the most ardent loyalty.

The Protestant movement bought into this, albeit in a very limited and special sense. It appealed to something that was sensible: the Bible. And it tended to allow a certain forgetfulness: namely, that the word of God refers to God—and that God cannot be taken as merely another fact in the universe of facts. We use the word "fact" today almost as a synonym for what is true. Actually, its root meaning (from Latin *factum*) is that of a thing done or a deed. From the perspective of an earlier way of thinking, a fact is "accidental" in the scholastic sense, and therefore something that participates in the truth, but is subordinate to essential truths. The older way thought it important that facts have no permanence; but essential truths—though unseen—never cease to be. The modern style of thinking actually reversed the sense of an ordered reality by allowing "facts" the priority and such things as principles, values, and virtues became hardly real at all.

At this point, the sword placed in the Reformers' hands became the weapon used to decapitate late medieval Scholasticism. Perhaps one of the inadvertent losses of the Protestant Reformation resulted from its zeal to separate itself from the "Sophists," as Reformers tended to call the Scholastics. Struggling to give revelation its proper place, they also lost (not at first, and never altogether, but at length) fifteen hundred years of Catholic intellectual tradition, a tradition that bothered itself with the *iotas*, and whether or not Mary should be referred to as the God-bearer (the *Theotokos*), and what precisely is the Pelagian error and what is not, and whether the two natures of Christ conflict with the unity of his person, and so on. Protestants also lost, in the bargain, a memory that these questions had really arisen from pastoral concerns, and were not merely the speculative preoccupations of scholars.

This was never Luther's intention. Yet he felt the need to slay the monster of "human reason" that had for some become an idol. His words, therefore, as those of the other Reformers, great and small, were those one articulates in battle. "But faith slaughters reason," he said, "and kills the beast that the whole world and all the creatures cannot kill." Luther used reason and learning: a fact not lost on his contemporaries. But once Scholasticism-gone-mad had been reined in, those words would have a different ring. In an exposition of Gal 3:6, Luther said that when faith killed reason in Abraham, it "sacrificed God's bitterest and most harmful enemy.... Thus devout people, by their faith, kill a beast that is greater than the world; and so they offer a highly pleasing sacrifice and worship to God."

Even the worst fundamentalist would be happy to give Luther the scholar an airing against the arrogance of modern scholarship. Yet modern Protestant churches suffer but little from Aristotelian logic nowadays, and university faculties do not suffer at the hands of the likes of John Scotus Erigena, or even a Peter Abelard. They perhaps stand more in danger from a class of intellectual "wreckers" who might even find some comfort in Luther's tilting against the dragon of Reason. Some see Protestantism as a triumph of Augustinian Christianity; and indeed it is rightly seen that way especially as regards the doctrine of salvation. Yet we find that Luther never troubled with the Trinity quite in the same way Augustine did, nor did Calvin trouble himself with the meaning of history as did the author of the *Civitas Dei*, and in reality treated history, especially the history of the Church, as a propagandist and not as a scholar.

Thus we look at the Protestant Reformation in one of two possible ways. One, I believe, does no real honor to the Reformers or to the movement of Protestant churches ever since. The other takes seriously the principle of *Ecclesia reformata sed semper reformanda* (the Church reformed, but always to be reformed).

First, we can see the Protestant movement, along with its evangelical continuation, as a rediscovery of a truth that was so valuable to the understanding of the gospel and the nature of salvation and the Church that it must be defended at all costs against every competing idea. Lest we fall back into the Pelagianism and near-idolatry of the Roman church of the Middle Ages (these words would be too mild for some folk), then we must stand firmly the ground marked *sola scriptum*, *sola gratia*, *sola fide*, and so on.

Or, second, we can see the Reformation as a correction made in the nick of time, at great cost to those who remained with the Western Church and those who left. It was a necessary correction in the course of the Church of Christ; when it had lost its North Star, the Reformation violently seized the helm and helped set it back on course. The intellectual tradition of the Sophists (alike criticized by the loyal Erasmus and the exiled Luther), along with other elements of church tradition, had drifted so far that it no longer convincingly centered on that which was revealed. The Church no longer heard so distinctly and convincingly the Word of God at the heart of her tradition.

Safeguarding a Truly Catholic Vision of the World

Now considerable time has passed. And the time comes to correct the correction. (Otherwise what is the meaning of *reformata sed semper reformanda?*) The zeal with which the Reformers elevated Scripture caused them for a time to mute the voices of that weighty preaching with which the church of antiquity had come to understand the meaning of Scripture. Not that Luther or Calvin neglected these ancient treasures, but others did, and those following in their train followed not the gentle new tack of the Reformers, but rather set eyes on the horizon and followed it. The councils, the creeds, the grand theologians, the apologists, and the philosophers—all could now be abandoned.

This was never the intention of the Reformers whom Pelikan called a "cadre of intellectuals." But the turn had been made, the rudder seized with such zeal and urgency that the course correction was taken by many in future generations to be the "course." Rather than following the gentle curve to deeper waters, some set course straight as an arrow to the horizon.

Perhaps now is the time, now that Protestants are noticing that something is seriously missing, to reach back and affirm a truly "catholic" tradition: one that did not deny philosophy but used it to the glory of God and for the sake of the Church. Post-Kantian cynicism about truth is an escape only for a church that has abandoned revelation as well as reason. Once the impossibility of reason has been granted, the black hole that is formed by that concession soon pulls revelation in after it.

In some ways already a reattachment of Protestant thinking to an earlier and broader tradition is going on, and in many places around the world. Pressed by the moral demands of our age, a number of institutes, public advocacy groups, and ad hoc interdenominational committees have taken steps to reach across the divide by going back to the sources. Those interests can also be seen in the programs of a number of newly established seminaries and divinity schools, as well as beachheads at older established institutions. There has been, of late, open derision directed against those "tradition-impaired" seminaries (as Thomas Oden has called them) that are still chasing the caprices of theological novelty or getting caught up with the whirling dervishes of ever more rarefied political interest groups.

Now is the time for evangelicals to declare themselves in a very intentional way for the recovery of intellectual aims that are unapologetically catholic—not as a way of losing their distinctiveness, but as a way of recovering the task that made the separation necessary in the first place: the safeguarding of a truly catholic vision of the world and its redemption.

3

Cloning and the Moral Imagination (1997)[1]

WHY DID NEWS OF "Dolly"—the lamb successfully produced by cloning in Scotland last February—so quickly change into a discussion of human medical ethics? Unlike animal breeding—a practice that could conceivably be transferred to the human situation, but doesn't normally evoke the concern that it will—the idea of cloning sends the imagination racing far beyond the competency of science and raises the specter of human reproduction using the same general principle. This happens despite the fact that, while selective breeding is a real possibility among human beings (though not an imminent probability), cloning is not yet even a technical possibility. In this case we have become concerned with possible realities even before reaching the point of real possibilities.

The question "Can it happen?" is a practical one, but it causes the imagination to pause only briefly, not to stop. For, in four hundred years of rapid technological advances, people have learned not to speculate that it can never happen. Too often the word "can't" is covered in the dust of speeding new technologies. Thus is the imagination fueled to make the now improbable leap from a ewe lamb to a human being. The mind easily converts from real possibilities among farm animals to possible realities among human beings. So whether or not cloning presents an ethical problem as it now exists, it presents a temptation on the level of the human imagination. The hint of such a possibility changes the probability of how we understand and value life.

1. Originally published in *Touchstone* 10.3 (Summer 1997).

Safeguarding a Truly Catholic Vision of the World

The ethical problems, at first remote and speculative, present themselves once we allow for three considerations:

First, without cloning, the emergence of life for all higher forms of animal life involves the contribution of two separate individuals. At the human level this implies relationship. Cloning allows us to imagine birth without relationship.

This is the obverse side, of course, of the age-old reluctance of the Church to sanction sexual relations without the possibility of procreation. The Roman Catholic Church has traditionally held out against artificial birth-control methods—methods that might encourage sex without discipline—because they seem to sever that necessary connection between the act of sex and the production of life. In recent years, several Protestant theologians and ethicists have raised similar questions. Stanley Hauerwas of Duke is one; and Albert Mohler of the Southern Baptist Theological Seminary is another.

Cloning, if it were possible for human beings, would break the connection in the other direction. Instead of sex without reproduction, it would be reproduction without sex (or even the idea of remote sexual cooperation, as in the case of artificial insemination). The idea of an individual who owes his biological existence to a single individual, and not to a sexually related pair of individuals, means that the genetic line is reduced from a web that spreads outward into the past—two parents, four grandparents, eight great-grandparents, and so on, embracing ancestors enough to populate whole cities—to a single strand (as the process might be imagined) that marches parallel to, but isolated from, all the rest of humanity.

In China a few years ago I gazed with wonder at the altar of a temple dedicated to a family's ancestors. On the lowest shelf were pictures of the recently deceased. A step up were photos of men and women from an era before World War II. A rank higher stood plaques with names of those a generation earlier, the great grandparents of the still living elders in the family. Three ranks higher still bore the names of, it seemed, a host of ancestors, all presided over by images of mythical patriarchs.

Just as reproduction from two individuals implies community; the replication of one implies isolation. In our age it is sometimes difficult to urge much angst over this prospect; but in earlier ages and in other places, the prospect is clearly understood as catastrophic.

Second, in nature, birth signals the solidarity of life when divergent beings—here we are not simply referring to number, but diversity—give life

Cloning and the Moral Imagination (1997)

to one that combines features of both. In birth, the two literally "become one flesh."

Cloning allows one to imagine the needlessness of diverse life forms. One genetically identical generation succeeds another. The process requires not diversity—two sexes, separate and distinct genetic make-up—but identity, one sex (as it stands now, female), and one genetic code. Distinction and cooperation (if that's what we can call sexual love) are replaced by equality and uniformity.

The very idea of human community requires a certain refined sentiment about the possibility of relating diverse individuals and a corporate unity—*e pluribus unum*. Sexual reproduction underscores this worldview, and one might imagine a world that valued collectivity instead of cooperation, uniformity rather than distinction—the homogenization of humanity.

Altogether apart from the real possibility of this prospect, the ethical issues emerge in the imagination, just as they did from Thomas More's imagining Utopia, Machiavelli's imagining the cunning tyranny of the Prince, Marx imagining the proletarian revolution and the disappearance of church and state, and certain Nazi scientists imagining a race purified through eugenics. Each of these took an imaginative leap into the future, a leap based upon intellectual and scientific advances. But the actions to which these scientific dreams gave rise were provoked not by the science, but by the dreams.

Third, in nature, birth makes vividly clear that life is a gift. We generally do not choose gifts, and to the extent that we do, it is that much less a gift. Instead a gift comes to us out of the will, imagination, and love of another person. What we receive in a new life is never altogether predictable. A parent may spend many unhappy years attempting to turn the gift of a child into something they would have chosen for themselves, but that wish is nearly always futile and often destructive. The life of another is a gift from God, in whatever unexpected form this life, this child, comes to us.

When Emily, our first child, was born, I remember being altogether knocked off balance by the very reality and particularity of this tiny child. I knew what a baby looked like. We were, after all, expecting—and in fact anxiously anticipating this moment. Resemblance to both my wife and me could be seen and was remarked on by our friends. But a weird question kept coming to mind: "Who is this child?" She was neither my wife nor me. She was alien—a stranger who we would have to get acquainted with, a guest who had never lived with us before. She was other than us—a matter she would remind us of forcefully in her teenage years—and because she was other than us, she was a gift to us.

Now raise the possibility of cloning. We become not the receivers of life, but we can at least imagine ourselves its manufacturers. The notion of "planned parenthood" takes on an even more depressingly sterile aspect than before. We often receive what does not at first especially please us; that is the nature of a gift. In the case of a child, our hearts almost miraculously make room for one who remains at first unknown to us. Do we imagine, or would we be tempted to imagine, that in cloning we short-circuit the life-giving and heart-enlarging shock of newness, otherness, and strangeness that accompanies the arrival of every child? Is there not the tendency in all of human associations to avoid this shock, to cultivate a society of those who look and act in a way that conforms to ourselves and those we already know, and furthermore to avoid those who are different? Is not genocide the extreme and violent manifestation of the very human wish to avoid that which is so obviously not "us?"

The questions raised, coincidentally, correspond to three values inherent in the Christian view of life: the distinction within life, the unity of life, and the givenness of life. As the Trinity combines distinction, unity, and self-giving, mutually receiving love, so the natural experience of birth seems to give daily witness to those same three qualities. The ethical must come to grips with those three.

4

The Changing Face of Baptist Theology (1998)[1]

A QUESTION ABOUT THE changing face of Baptist theology is one that moves, in time, from the past to the present and into the future. For when we specify Baptist theology we are linking that theology with a tradition, and it is not yet entirely settled (nor will it likely ever be) what is the precise character of that tradition. And when we ask about the changing face of Baptist theology we are assuming that it has not only a present but also a future. The interesting thing about the topic is that, although the shape of the Baptist tradition in theology and the shape of this brand of Christian thinking is a matter of great contention today—perhaps especially among Southern Baptists, the largest group of Baptists—many, even outside the denomination, predict that it will have an increasing influence in the future on the Christian community at large.[2]

Speculation regarding trends is risky in any area of human endeavor, it is perhaps especially so in theology, where the urgent questions of one day are replaced by the unexpected events, and the consequently new questions, of the next. But assuming our recent past is some indication of the theological concerns that will face us tomorrow, it is perhaps safe to say that Baptists must respond theologically on three fronts. First, we must face honestly and somewhat dispassionately the question, "What is our theological identity?" Does it emerge out of the Calvinistic tradition, the

---

1. Originally published in *Review and Expositor* 95 (1998): 21–38.
2. See, for instance, Marty, "Baptistification Takes Over."

tradition of the Radical Reformation, or some modification of one or the other? Second, a question that proceeds out of the first, "How do Baptists and their theology respond to the strain within modern Western culture and to the assessment that it has come to an end?" This question becomes more urgent if we assume that Baptist convictions about freedom and individualism (i.e., "soul competency"), as well as their democratic mode of church polity, make Baptists unalterably children of the modern age. And third, "Will a Baptist theological outlook be capable of contributing to a new sense of an ordering principle in the life of the church and society?" As the world necessarily searches for a means of creating order out of its long engagement with twentieth-century war and social conflict, will it turn to new authoritarian regimes, or will it turn to the kinds of mediating, local institutions, founded on transcendent rather than secular hopes, hopes that spring from the kind of theology that Baptists can, if they will, articulate? That Baptist theology might lend the world just such a lamp in the midst of a growing darkness is a matter for which we should both hope and pray.

Theology and the Baptist Tradition

While there are good reasons for thinking about Christianity in its broadest, most catholic form, the fact is that theology comes to us embodied in specific traditions that are distinct in important ways from one another. James William McClendon, Jr., is one who, to his great credit, resists the temptation to ignore the advantages of speaking out of a specifically Baptist tradition—or, as he prefers, the more inclusive baptist (lower case) tradition. He recognizes that to do so is no mere denominational provincialism. Rather it includes a large subsection of the Christian community that he maintains is part of the Radical Reformation, as distinct from Lutheran and Reformed. He identifies these baptist churches as those which others classify as "Free Church" or "Believers Church."[3]

Enumerating the marks of the Radical Reformation as "biblicism," (or, more pleasingly, he says later, "a recovery of the theology of the Bible"), "mission," "liberty," "discipleship," and "community," he expands the family of baptists to include more than those who bear the name. He includes, among others, "Disciples of Christ and Churches of Christ, Mennonites, Plymouth Brethren, Adventist, Russian Evangelicals, perhaps Quakers, certainly black Baptists (who often go by other names), the (Anderson,

3. McClendon, *Ethics*.

The Changing Face of Baptist Theology (1998)

Indiana) Church of God, Southern and British and European and American Baptists, the Church of the Brethren, perhaps some Methodists, Assemblies of God, associated intentional communities not organized as churches, missionary affiliates of all the above, and ... hundreds of other bodies."[4]

McClendon's inclusion of all these movements within Christianity in the baptist tradition rather than only those with Baptist nomenclature accords well with Martin Marty's contemporary observation that the "baptistification" of Christianity "takes up more and more of the Christian map."[5] Yet McClendon does more than argue for typical modes of religious expression; he implies, if not states outright, that such "marks" indicate a reliance on an Anabaptist tradition. He is convinced by the argument made by Glen Stassen, for one.[6] He is also joined by a number of studies undertaken by William Estep, including *The Anabaptist Story*, in which he argues that English Separatists of the sixteenth and seventeenth centuries were, on a number of fronts, influenced by the continental Anabaptist movement.[7] The mass of evidence he brings to advance the case is weighty and has been convincing to many. However, Estep is no mere propagandist; he is, in the first place, a careful scholar who does not hesitate to admit when the evidence is either indirect or must be severely qualified.[8] Over against

---

4. Ibid., 28–35.

5. Marty, "Baptistification Takes Over," 33.

6. McClendon, *Ethics*, 20; citing Stassen, "Anabaptist Influences in the Origin of the Particular Baptists."

7. Estep, *Anabaptist Story*, see especially 200–224. He ends with the summary statement, "Today the Anabaptist heritage is not the sole possession of some inconspicuous sect in the backwater of civilization. Rather it is the prized possession of every advanced civilization of the twentieth century world. Where men believe in the freedom of religion, supported by a guarantee of separation of church and state, they have entered into that heritage. Where men have caught the Anabaptist vision of discipleship, they have become worthy of that heritage" (224). The question arises here, of course, of whether such universal values as freedom, self-sacrifice, community, and so on, are in fact the product of a tradition so much as the product of many traditions that might arise independently of one another. The fact that neither the Anabaptists nor the Huguenots supported the oppressive measures of the rising nation- states might argue that these sentiments arose from a broader base than that of the Anabaptists alone—or even from the Anabaptists as major contributor—who, by the way, also were pacifists, a position not notably taken by the thousands of Baptists in Cromwell's New Model Army when it invaded Ireland!

8. Estep points out, for instance, that Robert Browne, who might have been influenced by Mennonite refugees in Norwich "explicitly denied any relationship with them" (202). He says that while many scholars admit an Anabaptist influence upon the English Separatist movement, disagreement exists among them on "the nature and extent of this influence" (202). He freely points out that not much material is available that

whatever argument might be made to the contrary, there is the consistent evidence that English Baptists denied their connections with Anabaptists because of attempts by their enemies in England to tar them with the same brush as that with which writers and speakers of the day colored the lurid accounts of the Munster atrocities in the sixteenth century as well as a number of other incidents on the Continent that caused most movements of the Reformed type to emphasize their distinctiveness.[9]

In addition there is the difficulty of treating an intellectual tradition as if it were a biological strain that must be traced back to a single mutant specimen. Is it not possible that Separatists, in launching their argument against the state church, would occasionally come upon arguments that sound remarkably Anabaptist? And could they not even use Anabaptist arguments, which they undoubtedly did, while differing with them on such central Anabaptist tenets such as "oaths, magistracy, and military service"?[10] And is it not probable that any number of groups, pressed by the Protestant argument for *sola scriptum*, would happen upon reasons for rejecting infant baptism, aligning themselves inadvertently with the Anabaptists on that particular point, as well as with the corollary argument against a state church, but hardly making of themselves an extension of the Anabaptist movement. The argument against strained efforts to link English and American Baptists in some kind of historical necessity to the Anabaptists is countered with effortless prose by the distinguished historian Barrington White:

---

gives us knowledge of the doctrinal positions of the first Separatist conventicles, of those arrested in the 1550s, of why the early Separatists were accused of Pelagianism ("could imply," he writes, "a rejection of infant baptism; but the question of infant baptism was not mentioned"). Much generally points to ideas and doctrines similar to those of the Anabaptists, but again they are ideas widely held by Protestants and not those specifically or uniquely held by Anabaptists.

9. White, *English Baptists of the Seventeenth Century*, 68.

10. These exceptions, as McBeth points out in *Baptist Heritage*, 95, show up, for instance, in a response from General Baptist churches known as the "Tookey correspondence" as early as 1624, indicating that while the early movement in England was willing to adopt some of the Anabaptist arguments on specific points, it is certainly difficult to see that they are carrying forward the heritage of the Continental Anabaptists. These views would be shared by scholars such as William Whitsitt, Henry Dexter, William Whitley, R. G. Torbet, Norman Maring, Winthrop Hudson, W.G. McLoughlin, B. R. White, and Robert Baker who, as McBeth summarized the argument, "minimize Anabaptist influence before 1600, and . . . are more impressed with Baptist/ Anabaptist differences than similarities," 49.

First, it was entirely possible for both groups to come independently to the same conclusions about the essential nature of the Christian Church because they both shared the frequent Protestant tendency to appeal to the Bible as providing the one unchanging pattern or blueprint for the faith. Secondly, even if the Separatists did learn anything from the Anabaptists they were highly unlikely to admit this for two reasons: first, because they were always concerned to emphasize that their convictions were derived directly from the Bible and not from traditions of men and, secondly, because they would know that to quote the Anabaptists as a source for any idea was a quick way in both the 16th and 17th centuries to close men's minds to its acceptance. Thirdly, there does exist, in the records of the evolution of the English Separatists, a plausible explanation of the development of their views which does not require the introduction of "Anabaptist" influence.[11]

Others argue strongly for the Calvinistic influence among Baptists in the early days of British and American Baptists. They have the advantage of much more apparent evidence for this view of Baptist heritage and, unless one is prepared to argue that Reformed language and doctrinal formulation of nearly three centuries merely covers up a deeper layer of "true Baptist origins," the argument lies not in chance encounters and fortuitous parallels in language, but in explicit statements of Baptist theologians and confessions. Thomas J. Nettles, for instance, can argue from the evident Calvinism of the Particular Baptist London Confession of 1644, and the even more pointedly Calvinist nature of the Second London confession of 1677. These statements, along with the Savoy Confession and the Westminster Confession, evidently came from a common stock of doctrinal expression. The words of the 1644 Confession and its successors are suggestive of the *Institutes* and not at all of, for instance, of the early Anabaptist Schleitheim Confession. This is true not only in the ordinary sense of common vocabulary and system, but also in regard to the tone and the habitual focus. Again, Nettles can point to the undisguised Reformed theology of John Gill, Charles Haddon Spurgeon, Andrew Fuller, Isaac Backus, Richard Furman, Basil Manly, Sr., James Petigru Boyce, and quite a number of others who were powerfully instrumental in the doctrinal expression of Baptists through the middle part of the nineteenth century.[12]

---

11. White, *English Baptists of the Seventeenth Century*, 22. See also the argument presented in White, *The English Separatist Tradition*.

12. See Nettles, *By His Grace and for His Glory*.

Safeguarding a Truly Catholic Vision of the World

Timothy George has made the case that the practice of believers' baptism is not simply an alien doctrine fused with the Calvinism of English Separatists and Puritans, but was a doctrine actually strengthened in the theological environment of Reformed thought. The practice of believers' baptism and the case against paedobaptism would clarify the relationship between *sola gratia* and *sola fide*. He indicates that one might trace the Reformed argument for adult baptism from Thomas Patient's 1654 work, *The Doctrine of Baptism and the Distinction of the Covenants*, to Karl Barth's *Church Dogmatics* (IV/4).[13] The Magisterial Reformers, George points out, were plagued by their own inconsistencies with regard to the doctrine of baptism, wanting perhaps not to invite the greater disapproval that was reserved for the Anabaptists. The Reformed Baptists who later took up this unattended part of the Protestant agenda were able to press the case of linking faith and grace further. "If the Reformed doctrine of believers' baptism shares with Luther a firm commitment to the coinherence of baptism and faith, it also resonates strongly with Zwingli and Calvin on the unity of God's people through the ages, [for] baptism in the name of the Father, Son, and Holy Spirit points not only to the sovereignty of God in salvation . . . but also to the eschatological fulfillment of that covenant in the incarnate Christ and the calling forth of his body, the church."[14]

While there are those who wish to recover the Reformed theology that characterized Baptist thought through most of the eighteenth and nineteenth centuries, there is also the temptation to see Baptists as hewing the line more closely than they ever did, and some have given in, on occasion, to the temptation to burden Baptist theology with an ideological mission determined by an idealized Reformed system. To his credit, George has not treated the historical Calvinism of Baptists as simply an ideological point of departure and has shown no signs of wanting (as others might have wished of him) to create a sort of new Baptist etiological myth. Witness, for instance, his slight discomfort with Thomas Nettles' failure to bring a certain nuanced argument regarding the development of Calvinist theology in its connection with Baptist history.[15] Whether George, as well as Nettles and others, have given due attention, and allowed for enough emphasis upon, other influences upon Baptist, and even those occasions where Baptists have brought something relatively new to Reformed thought, is another question.

13. George, "Reformed Doctrine of Believers' Baptism," 246.
14. Ibid., 250.
15. George, Review of *By His Grace and for His Glory*, 143.

If we are to proceed beyond the impasse of Baptists claiming an Anabaptist heritage, along with all its features which obviously never belonged in any proper sense to English and American Baptists (a claim which, it appears, dies the death of a thousand qualifications) and beyond those claiming Reformed antecedents, and are thereby tempted to exaggerate the precise dosage of Baptist Reformed thinking, we must give more attention to the features of Baptist thought that are exactly *not* in harmony with Reformed thought as it typically developed in Europe and among English Puritans. We would do this not in order to disclaim what is abundantly obvious, namely the Baptist debt to Calvinism, but in order to see more clearly what new gifts the Baptist way brought to Reformed Christianity and, more broadly, to Protestant Christianity.

R. W. Southern wrote in his history of medieval culture of a remarkable discovery concerning the Rule of St. Benedict. It was long thought that Benedict was the original author of that rule. But, as it turns out, the Rule itself, in its basic form, was much older. What Benedict did, however, was to shape and adapt the Rule in such a way that what was originally a severe code that would have been useful only under very limited and rare circumstances was made into a more general guide that could adapt itself to broad and varied circumstances. "Despite the rigor of the regime, the Rule is written as if it were designed for all men everywhere."[16] So while the Rule itself was important, it was the slight but strategic changes that made the enormous difference, and it was because of these changes that the Rule, the Dominican Order itself, and the monastic movement became a major cultural force in Western Christendom. What made it so was not the broad outlines of the monastic rule, but the subtle shaping that gave it a certain life and practicality and that enabled it to last for hundreds of years. In a similar way we might think of the Baptist adoption of Reformed thought, not as slavishly shackled to the Canons of Dort, but as the medium by which Baptists made their own, and perhaps superior, contribution to Protestant Christianity.

Did the early Particular Baptist movement adopt a Calvinist doctrine, but only after "shaping" it in this way? One must remember, of course, that the Calvinist system at its source is one thing and the development of a theological school is quite another. So the Calvinist tradition that had influenced so much of Protestantism was continually in flux, taking upon itself remarkable changes in the regions it influenced, whether France and

---

16. Southern, *Western Society and the Church in the Middle Ages*, 220.

the Netherlands, or Scotland and England. Baptists were both inheritors of and contributors to these changes; and as we trace certain forces within Reformed thought, both Baptist and otherwise, we discover a certain softening that moves in a very different direction than the Synod of Dort's sharp reaction to Arminian theology (the source of the well known "five points" formulation of Calvinism).

Tracing this movement down to American, and more specifically Southern Baptists, we can find four circumstances that moved Reformed doctrine in a direction that began to allow space for humanity, rationality, free agency, and faith. To put the matter in terms of a classical theological tension, Christians have always had to balance the doctrines of Creation and Redemption. To the extent that creation is good, the necessity of redemption fades. To the extent that the need of redemption is felt, creation is seen as having lost its goodness. Pelagianism puts so much trust in the good creation that it forgets the need of redemption through grace. Gnosticism, at the other extreme, is all redemption and no (good) creation. In Europe, under the spell of Calvinist Christianity, Arminianism seemed to invite the Pelagian error, and hyper-Calvinism the Gnostic error. Within this struggle, Baptists pushed toward the acknowledgment of God's good creation by virtue of the human willl being capable of choosing freely, even though some Baptists even seemed to forget that that is what the practice of believers' baptism inevitably implied. Over the course of time we see this push toward creation and a natural theology in four stages.

(1) We see it in the influence of the Baptist expression of Reformed thought that is found in the early London Confession, clearly enough in the earlier 1644 confession, but even more markedly in the confessions of 1677 and 1688. In the Doctrine of God and the Doctrine of Sin, the articles are little differentiated from those of the Savoy Confession, a contemporary document, and they anticipate the Westminster Confession. When it comes to the doctrine of election, of providence, and of the church, one begins to notice the peculiar Baptist insistence on the privilege of men and women to choose freely, not according to tradition, nor according to coercive authority, but according to individual conscience. The gospel is to be preached to all, and there is no explicit teaching of reprobation.

(2) In America, the Second Great awakening had a remarkable influence on most Protestants, but perhaps none more so than the Baptists. The entire period, from 1800 to 1835, had an enormous influence upon American

life; but, in specific regard to churches, it moved the Calvinist tradition, as James Tull said, "in the direction of Arminianism."[17]

It is also interesting that when New England Calvinism with its strong emphasis upon God's sovereignty, turned—as its logical extreme inevitably would—toward the monist position (i.e., toward unitarianism), it was the revivalist Calvinism of Nathaniel Taylor that most effectively countered this heresy.[18] The biographer of Taylor, Sydney Mead, says that revivals were not so much the province of the "Consistent Calvinists," but that of the "Baptists and Methodists, and, in general, the 'Enthusiasts.'" The effects of this revivalism, however, with its emphasis upon the individual freely turning toward God, was the strengthening of Calvinist Christianity against the "infidels and Unitarians."[19]

(3) The influence of Scottish common sense philosophy, which sought to give place to the human capacity for knowing and understanding the world, moved Reformed thought still further from the hyper-Calvinism associated with the Synod of Dort. Scottish Realism was a reaction against Enlightenment idealism, taking on by implication, if not always expressly, the methods of Descartes, Locke, Berkeley, and Hume. The writings of Thomas Reid and Dugald Stewart were used widely in American universities and seminaries and had the effect of tempering the tendency in Calvinist theology of the strictest sort to denigrate human reason. This philosophy became "the great offensive weapon of New England apology as well as its great instrument of constructive reasoning."[20] It allowed Taylor, for instance, to correct for the excesses in Jonathan Edwards' philosophy that would make the human response to God's act of grace unintelligible. "Moral agents," he said, "are the proximate efficient causes of their own acts." That does not make them the ultimate cause, but it does mean that there is, along this line of thought, reason for saying that the free choice of responsible adults is the basis upon which the covenant between human being and God is established. One does not have to exercise the imagination much to see how this reasoning fits well with the Baptist claim for believers' baptism. Among Baptists it is not surprising to find, therefore, that Francis Wayland, president of Brown University and the author of

17. Tull, "Evangelicals and Baptists," 5
18. See Mead, *Nathaniel William Taylor*, 95–127.
19. Ibid., 124.
20. Foster, *Genetic History of the New England Theology*, 246.

America's first textbook in moral philosophy—the one most widely used in American colleges throughout the nineteenth century—was influenced by this school of thought.[21]

Although Scottish Realism was conspicuous in New England and at Princeton, it was particularly influential in the South where, coincidentally, the larger part of the Baptists were to be found after the first two decades of the nineteenth century. James Farmer pointed out:

> The Scottish philosophy enjoyed a broad appeal in the United States, but it was particularly popular among the Southern clergy. Its influence can be traced in the careers of Presbyterians John Holt Rice at Hampton-Sydney, David Caldwell at the University of North Carolina, Moses Waddell at Willington Academy in South Carolina and the University of Georgia, Jonathan Maxcy and James Thornwell at the South Carolina College and Columbia Seminary, Robert Lewis Dabney at Union Seminary in Richmond, and Robert J. Breckinridge at Danville (Kentucky) Seminary. Common Sense was also widely adopted by the Methodists. Nathan Bangs recommended the philosophy as an antidote to "the errors of Locke."[22]

One has only to mention the fact that, since Witherspoon, Scottish Realism was the official philosophy of nineteenth-century Princeton, where Charles Hodge taught James Petigru Boyce and through him influenced an entire generation of Baptists in the South in their most formative period. It is likely, however, that even without Boyce the Baptist clergy would have felt the effects of a philosophy so widely adopted in their region among most Protestant teachers of theology and ministers of the gospel.

(4) Moving now to the early years of the twentieth century we find that the theology of E. Y. Mullins with its emphasis upon human experience is not precisely a departure from earlier theology as it had developed in the South and among Baptists, but it can be seen as a continuation of the trend marked out from Taylor to Hodge, and passed on extensively to the generation of Baptists in the nineteenth century. It was a trend influenced both by the American revivals and by Scottish Realism to look to the human consciousness for an understanding of Christian truth without abandoning the primacy of revelation. It should not be surprising that E. Y. Mullins could find elements within Schleiermacher's work which were helpful to his own

21. Ibid., xxiii.
22. Farmer, *Metaphysical Confederacy*, 98.

thinking; Schleiermacher's romanticism was after all—like the Scottish philosophy—a reaction against the excesses of Enlightenment rationalism. One can be sure, however, that for Mullins experience was ruled by revelation, not the other way around. In that, he was always closer to Calvin than to Schleiermacher.[23]

How does one respond, then, to these varied attempts to root Baptist theology in its proper tradition? The identity of Baptist theology is likely not to be found in some contrived founding myth of anabaptist roots—whether that be of the nineteenth-century "trail of blood" variety or of the twentieth-century attempt to find a radical Protestant fountainhead that would exorcise the conservatism of the Southern Baptist Convention in its post nineteen-seventies form. Nor will it be found in a kind of Calvinist revival that fails to appreciate the subtle forces that both attracted Baptists to the Reformed expression of theology and that allowed them to act upon that tradition in a way uniquely suited to their understanding of the Scriptures. Instead, it will likely be found in a Reformed theology so articulated that it gives adequate place to human experience and, at the same time, serves to underline the false stratagems of modern culture as well as to affirm what is worthy in that culture. A theology of this type must accommodate the Baptist conviction that (to use Mullins's term) the soul is "competent" to respond to God's gift of himself in Jesus Christ. At the same time, it must recover the communal implications of a church composed of those called out by Christ and freely consenting to his yoke of obedience.

---

23. Thomas Nettles' evaluation of Mullins is that, while attempting to counter the liberal theology that was winning the day in America of the turn of the century, he actually conceded the rigorously theocentric nature of Southern Baptist theology as represented by Dagg and Boyce, and attempted to reconstruct theology on the basis of religious experience "producing the gradual theological shift of Southern Baptists from a thoroughgoing Calvinism to semi-Arminianism." See *By His Grace and For His Glory*, 264. He seems not to account for the subtle changes in Calvinism, especially in America, during the nineteenth century—changes that made it very difficult at points to say what a "thoroughgoing Calvinism" was, and in any event, one could be sure that it was some distance from either the canons of Dort or even from what would be called a Kuyperian Calvinism. Mullins' turn toward experience was nothing like a break from the immediate past in view of the strong influences of American revivals and Scottish realism, and both of these (in America at least) were pressed toward a stronger emphasis upon human experience in theology by the Socinian errors of the New England Unitarianism.

Safeguarding a Truly Catholic Vision of the World

Baptists and the End of Modernity

James McClendon finds in the "baptist" tradition hope for reconstructing a theology that begins with a way of living and builds to the story of God's way among us. As a leading representative of a number of theologians and pastors who have adopted this mode of theology, McClendon recognizes the necessity of working our way out of a certain predisposition for which we have been trained as "modern" thinkers. The reason baptists have produced so little theology to date, he argues, is that the approach so natural to the baptist faith is hindered by Enlightenment, or modern, prescriptions for the way one must do theology. "The baptists in all their variety and disunity failed to see in their own heritage, their own way of using Scripture, their own communal practices and patterns, their own guiding vision, a resource for theology unlike the prevailing scholasticism round about them."[24]

The critique of modernity is nothing new. From Nietszche to Leo Strauss there has been the sometimes sad, sometimes exultant, realization that the modern project is one that has abandoned God. God is irrelevant, dead, or both. Without its moderate form, however, this style of thought would never have made its way out of the Salons of Paris and Berlin. The moderate Enlighteners—Locke, Kant, and others—shared the skepticism of Reimarus and Voltaire but not the antagonism to orthodox faith. Still, the hallmark of the Enlightenment was its reliance on reason and not revelation; on the free individual and not the society and culture; on the possibilities of the future and not the givenness of the past and tradition. The result has been that, while post-Enlightenment men and women might believe in God, divine revelation, creation, and miracles, they sense (and their culture fully enforces this sense) that their convictions, their arguments, and their values, are taken seriously only to the extent that they do not rely upon these categories of metaphysical transcendence. And, while even reason itself must be suspended at this point, they feel they must act as if they are responsible for their own being, that they are self-created and self-creating, and have need neither of tradition nor revelation, the former tying them to the community of other human beings and the latter illuminating their place in the order of existence itself.

Historically, the result of the skepticism fostered by the radical Enlightenment had been several kinds. First was the capitulation of the claims of the Enlightenment, but then an attempt to use the methods of the

---

24. McClendon, *Ethics*, 26.

The Changing Face of Baptist Theology (1998)

Enlightenment to establish a "reasonable" faith; Kant and Locke are classic examples of this approach. Second was the attempt to face squarely the implications of Enlightenment thought and struggle instead with the implications of the death of God; such was the approach of Nietszche and modern existentialists such as Camus and Sartre. This second deposition, which seemed to descend upon the West in the nineteenth-century, opened the flood gates for ideologies that offered alternate ways of ordering existence, since a transcendent point of reference was no longer available; notable among these are Marxism, fascism, various kinds of racism, psychoanalysis, and even capitalism as an ideological touchstone (rather than as merely an economic development). A third reaction took the form of surviving (and often flourishing) sentiments that the world is after all knowable in a limited sense, and its rational order might be discerned by analogy; in evidence of this, one must be struck by the resilience of Thomism in its various incarnations, Scottish realism, and the reconstruction of order represented in philosophy by Eric Voegelin, in political theory by Gerhart Niemeyer, in criticism by Marion Montgomery, in the arts by Flannery O'Conner and Walker Percy. Among Baptists, E. Y. Mullins and Millard Erickson would be principal figures in this kind of response.

Yet a fourth reaction to Enlightenment mentality is a Christian apologetic that takes the form of a critique of the Enlightenment's most obvious axiomatic features. Carl F. H. Henry might be taken as an example of this approach among Baptists as would Albert Mohler.[25] And a fifth response is one which might include such Baptist thinkers as McClendon, Nancey Murphy, and Stanley Grenz. As a reaction to modernity—and as a constructive attempt to go beyond modernity, to recognize a superseding era—this "postmodernism" is, of course, much broader than Baptists and, in fact, much broader than Christian. What makes it suspect in the first place, in the minds of some, is that the major European and North American proponents appear to be as aggressively anti-Christian as those of the radical Enlightenment three centuries ago.

As things have developed in recent years among Baptist theologians, it is the fifth response to modernity that has generated the greatest reaction,

25. Mohler, in fact, worries that evangelicals have adopted the thought patterns of modernity, which is essentially "the denial of the God of classical theism as sovereign, transcendent, omnipotent, and omniscient." (See Mohler, "The Eclipse of God at Century's End," 9). It is perhaps important that he does not see himself as allied with others who also claim to be reacting to modernity, and, who might be setting the theological agenda today for Evangelicalism.

and perhaps held for some the most promise of a constructive alternative to modern habits of mind. The writers of "Reenvisioning Baptist Identity: A Manifest for Baptist Communities in North America" contend that the kinds of discussions taking place among Baptists and among ideologues of the Left and the Right occur under the spell of distinctly modern assumptions that in fact are now wearing thin and are becoming increasingly irrelevant to the times we face. "Ideologies and theologies of the right and left, as different as they may appear," they write, "are really siblings under the skin by virtue of their accommodation to modernity and its Enlightenment assumptions."[26] It is clear from earlier versions of the letter that its target was the Moderate (Southern) Baptist discussion of a Baptist's "four fragile freedoms" popularized in the writings of Walter Shurden, which the writers evidently considered too uncritically dependent on the Enlightenment's idea of the autonomous individual. A second target was "Constantinian" efforts to create an alliance with political powers by those in the Southern Baptist Convention who manifested a broader worship of power *per se*. "What these agendas call freedom is what the gospel calls bondage to the false gods of nationalism, classism, or narcissism."[27]

Stanley Grenz has perhaps done the most to spell out the meaning of this postmodern critique of modernity and to demonstrate how this point of view can be accommodated to the gospel. In response to Foucault, Derrida, and Rorty— three of the most prominent philosophers of postmodernism—he rejects their rejection of objective truth, of that which lies outside the narrative of the Christian community—the metanarrative. At the same time Grenz adopts the postmodern critique of the Enlightenment—of its view of human knowledge as certain, objective, and the source of the good. It was such confidence in the triumph of reasonable knowing in a knowable world that caused Enlightenment-influenced societies to be marked by individualism, rationalism, dualism in the sense of separation of mind and matter, and noeticentrism. Such changes, Grenz says, calls for response:

> In the opinion of many, our society is in the throes of a monumental transition, the movement from modernity to postmodernity. For better or worse, the emerging generation—those who belong

---

26. Taken from the May, 1997 (final) version of the statement written by Mikael Broadway, Curtis Freeman, Barry Harvey, James Wm. McClendon, Jr., Elizabeth Newman and Philip Thompson, and signed by 55 Baptists including a number of the denomination's most notable theologians.

27. Ibid.

to the world of *Star Trek: The Next Generation* and its successors—is imbued with many aspects of the postmodern mind. Our task is not to defend modernism, to turn the intellectual tide back to the Enlightenment. Rather, we are called to understand the new intellectual climate, to view it through Christian eyes.[28]

Grenz, who is Professor of Baptist Heritage, Theology, and Ethics at Carey Theological College in Vancouver, has presented a clear evaluation of postmodernity and its influence on theology. Like Hans Frei and George Lindbeck before him, he has seen the postmodern impulse as more of an opportunity than a threat to the Christian way of thinking and living. And although theology had accommodated Enlightenment thought for most of the last two centuries, it need not be captive to that style of thought, and it need not sink along with ship-wrecked modernity with its individualism that has lost community and its mind that has lost its body, or its science that has lost the earth itself. "At the heart of the Enlightenment experiment," writes Grenz in his agenda-setting proposal for Evangelicals, "is the authority of reason . . . this entails a claim to dispassionate knowledge, [the] ability to . . . peer at the world from a vantage point outside the flux of history." In addition, it is optimistic, "spurred by a belief in inevitable progress." In contrast:

> Postmodern thinkers have given up the assumptions that reason has no limitations, that knowledge is inherently good and that we can solve all our problems. In response to the compartmentalization characteristic of the modern worldview, the watchword of postmodernity is holism—the desire to put back together what modernity has torn asunder. But of great significance for us is a related far-reaching change now transpiring. Postmodernism questions the radical individualism to which modernism gave birth and which has formed a hallmark of modern Western culture.[29]

For Nancey Murphy both the quest of modernity and its undoing has been the search for epistemological foundations. A world reduced to abstract reason must find a starting point, a foundation on which to build. And if indeed this is the story of the modern philosophy, then she concludes that it has been a sad story:

> Ideas that were clear and distinct to Descartes appear to others hopelessly vague or just plain false Empirical foundations have proven to be less troublesome in themselves, but here the

---

28. Grenz, *Primer on Postmodernism*, 17.
29. Grenz, *Revisioning Evangelical Theology*, 15.

problem of construction looms large. David Hume showed that from a foundation in immediate experience, no solid (deductive) conclusions could be drawn regarding anything but immediate experiences. So there appears to be an epistemological corollary of Murphy's law at work: whenever the foundations are suitably indubitable, they will turn out to be useless for justifying any interesting claims; when we do find beliefs that are useful for justifying the rest of the structure, they always turn out to be questionable.[30]

Thus an epistemological foundation gives abstract reason the leverage by which to explain the world; such power to reason gives the individual freedom from the necessities of the world; and such independence makes for a world of isolated and narcissistic individuals, undermines community, and subverts the rightful human claims of the senses and affections. That the contemporary world experiences such troubles is hardly in doubt. That Grenz's postmodernism or Murphy's rejection of epistemological foundations offer both the needed corrective and the way to a better mode of theologizing is put to the test by James McClendon's efforts to frame a theological approach that is more holistic than Enlightenment methods allowed, and more willing to begin rather than end with ethics. The test of this nonfoundational theology, according to Nancey Murphy, will be its capacity for "displayed coherence, fidelity to Scripture, and apt response to the experiences of human life that this way represents."[31]

James McClendon argues that the weakness of modern theology among Baptists (he cites Strong as an example) is that it is assumed that "foundations" should be examined first, whereupon doctrine is constructed, and finally ethics can be discovered from the outworking of doctrine. The implication is that the "logical order" is foundations—doctrine—ethics. To this he replies: "I will argue that it is not . . . the modern dream from Descartes and Locke onwards of philosophy as an ultimate intellectual umpire, telling ethics and religion what can and cannot be validly believed, is increasingly seen to be empty."[32] It is Richard Rorty's book, *Philosophy and the Mirror of Nature*, that he cites as an argument for the vanity of such modern dreams. He proposes that ethics should be taken up first (given chronological priority, but not logical priority—since "none has that").[33] By

30. Murphy, "Introduction," 11.
31. Ibid., 18–19.
32. McClendon, *Ethics*, 41–42.
33. Ibid., 42.

such an approach the Christian way can be understood from its narrative, a narrative that necessarily involves community as its source and its context, and a narrative that conveys not abstract reasoning alone, but the character, the passions, and the hopes of the whole person.

Baptist Vision and the Ordering Task of Theology

That new trends in theology "without foundations" or of a "postmodern" mode have captured the imagination of many thoughtful Baptists (or baptists) is evident from the energy these trends have gained over the recent years. The efforts among Baptists are supported by the realization that Anabaptist communities were not so intentionally theological as they were committed to living out the calling of those separated from the world as witnesses to the life of the gospel—an approach standing in contrast to the magisterial reformers and their concern to engage in a theological exchange with the church-at-large and the world-at-large. Whether the new experiments in theology are of lasting importance remains to be seen. The "radical theology" of the sixties, the "situation ethics" of the seventies, and the "liberation theologies" that crested in the eighties, have come and (almost) gone, leaving only the vague sentiments and the ideologies that supported their claims in the first place. Whether one can think through theology without logic—or, in other words, without some axiomatic ordering of concepts at the level of method—seems risky, although it doubtless appeals to the imagination. Baptists responsible for doing some theological reflection in the churches and universities, and who do this out of a sense of responsibility for the care of souls and the life of the church should approach these matters with a teachable spirit. But at the same time, no beneficial theology takes place without a willingness to assess critically the method being proposed.

Clarity in viewing the future of theology—as with any other kind of reflection regarding human life and thought—comes with facing the difficult questions that a new approach might present. In this case, difficult questions open the way to a new understanding of some very old principles, leaving us with the vivid impression that sometimes the way forward is to recall what we had almost forgotten. Several of these troubling questions suggest themselves in the midst of current discussion.

Safeguarding a Truly Catholic Vision of the World

1. Should we view the theologies of Baptists such as those of Grenz and McClendon as critiques of modernity, that is, as attempts to reinterpret the Christian gospel in the light of some kind of successor age to the modern one? There is, in the first place, the problem of nomenclature. Grenz uses the term "postmodern" intentionally and unapologetically, although it is clear that he remains troubled by the relativism of those who have become sources of postmodern thought—Foucault, Derrida, and Rorty—and by introducing the concept of "metanarrative" he seems to have sensed the inherent instability of a "narrative" theology. McClendon does not use the term postmodern often, perhaps because of the possibility that it creates more confusion than clarity, but like the postmodernists, he rejects the idea of logical foundations as the necessary starting point of theology. David Burrell saw McClendon and Smith's work *Understanding Religious Convictions* as a work anticipating postmodernism.[34] Both Grenz and McClendon stress the theological necessity of community, practice, and a narrative conveyance of discussion about God, categories clearly intended to counter the Enlightenment emphasis on individualism, abstraction, and reasoning.

2. But what about those features so frequently given as the marks of Enlightenment sentiment? Are the theologies of McClendon and Grenz, the philosophical critiques of Murphy, and the proposals of "Re-envisioning Baptist Identity" setting themselves truly against the legacy of the modern age—now coming to an untidy end—when they engage in the assumption that the Enlightenment is the source of individualism, which in turn has destroyed a sense of community? Or when they set their sights on "reason"—when in fact they must mean "reason as it came to be defined by Descartes and Locke," although they never qualify it in this way? It was Kant who penned the now famous motto of the Enlightenment, "Have the courage to use your own intelligence!" But is it only reason and individualism that this implies?

With regard to individualism, for instance, others reason that the Enlightenment and the modern age were no more than one segment in a very long arc of the pendulum swing. Ever since the Mediterranean world emerged from its mythopoetic collective consciousness under the influence of Greek philosophy, the Hebrew prophets, and the rise of Christianity, it has been marked by a deepened sense of the dignity of the individual. The writings of Eric Voegelin, Gerhart Niemeyer, Bruno Snell, Francis Fukuyama,

---

34. Burrell, "Convictions and Operative Warrant," 44.

and others have underscored both the strength of the movement and its tendency to invite gnostic-like theologies and pseudo-myths. Yet it is clear that neither the growing regard for the dignity of the individual person, nor the distortion and isolation to which such values are subject, began with the Enlightenment or with the modern age.

A similar point must be made about reason. While it is true that a new confidence in reason emerged, and that it was viewed as the power by which men and women would extricate themselves from the burden of tradition or necessity or divine laws, yet the seventeenth century could only have convincingly proposed such a role for human reason because already, going back to the height of medieval culture, a huge ecumenical movement centered around the recovery of Aristotelian thought had taken place through the labors of Alfarabi, Avicenna, Averroes, Maimonides, and Thomas Aquinas.

It seems, in a word, that neither individualism nor rationalism—those two marks of the modern age that gave justification to a cry for political, religious, and personal freedom—find their roots in the Enlightenment period, the period that postmodern critics wish to fault for its exaggerated stress upon, yes, individualism and rationalism. Consequently, Grenz, wishing to give postmodernity its due, calls for a gospel embodied in "a manner that is post-individualistic, post-rationalistic."[35] Yet such analysis ought to raise the question of whether that which has created such strains and such forebodings with regard to modernity has been rightly identified.

Of those who have joined in the general complaint about modernity, it is true that Foucault rejected the Enlightenment's assumption of an objective body of knowledge and its consequent rationalism as well as its individualism. Derrida similarly saw in language a self-referential attempt to empower or to divest of power, not an attempt to discover meaning. And Richard Rorty finds that, since it is "impossible to find a starting point for our discourse,"[36] and since transcendental authority for our actions or our discourse is out of the question, we are thrown back on the pragmatic project of shaping our own community. Yet such dilemmas and such projects become a concern primarily, if not exclusively, to those who have adopted the skepticism of the Enlightenment, which means (in principle, at least) working without the notion of creation, revelation, and the supernatural. It is difficult to know why such strictures would be of interest to Christian thinkers.

35. Grenz, *Primer on Postmodernism*, 167.
36. Ibid., 157.

3. Baptists won over by the postmodern quarrel with the Enlightenment have not, however, listened closely enough to other voices who would contend that our argument with modernity takes place on altogether different grounds. In this case, the enemy of our enemy is not necessarily our friend. What we might have learned from the labors of Eric Voegelin and Gerhart Niemeyer as well as (to an extent) Leo Strauss, and certainly Richard Weaver, is that the underlying impulse of modernity was to reject the "givenness," the irreducible limits and obligations of human life. If they were rationalists, like their medieval forebears, it was for the purpose of becoming through the exact sciences "*maîtres et possesseurs de la nature*" (Descartes). If they discovered the dignity of the individual, it was to follow the lead of those like Pico della Mirandella who wished to lift the human lot above the strictures of divine law and nature's necessity. The impulse of the Enlightenment cannot be adequately circumscribed with words like "individualism" and "rationalism," but must be seen as the ancient hope to be delivered from necessity and to be free in the sense of one who is autonomous (a law unto oneself) and thus self-created. This (as it seems to me) weightier critique of the Enlightenment sees that it springs from much deeper sources. Furthermore, the postmodern impulse, it seems, is to throw overboard only those features of the Enlightenment that are both its most superficial features and its most laudatory ones. In following the critique of Foucault and others, Grenz and other Baptist commentators who follow a postconservative line (as Grenz and some others have named it, paralleling the "postliberal" nomenclature of George Lindbeck) have missed the fact that these thinkers are most anxious to preserve that part of Enlightenment disposition that is most antagonistic to Christianity. Rorty, for instance, says, "Our identification with our community—our society, our political tradition, our intellectual heritage—is heightened when we see this community as ours rather than nature's, shaped rather than found."[37] We and our society, with its understanding of the reality in which it lives, are self-created. How different from the view that, even as life emerges from mystery, we are given the wherewithal to receive with thanksgiving and enjoyment a God-created nature, and we are illumined on our way by a God who makes himself known. In this case, nature, tradition, and revelation are given, not invented; and we are creatures, not creators. Seen in this way, postmodernists want to throw overboard the superficial furniture of the Enlightenment, but they want to save the boat itself. For the heart of the

---

37. Rorty, *Consequences of Pragmatism*, 166.

matter is the question whether God is acknowledged as God, or whether we wish to be our own gods. It was remarkable to me that Grenz did not recognize and comment upon the close connection between Nietzsche's lament that "If there is no God anything is permissible" and Jacques Derrida's comment (which he quoted) that "The absence of a transcendental signified extends the domain and the play of significations infinitely."[38]

4. In their attempt to find an alternative to the modernist's "reason" and develop a narrative theology, have the proponents actually resorted to what is neither reason nor narrative? Millard Erickson, while carefully underscoring all that "postconservatives" proposed to do, finds that their principal failing is in not demonstrating that it can be done. One must do more than merely assert the narrative nature of the gospel. Erickson asks, "What sort of language is used in discussing various types of language, or what paradigm is being followed when one discusses paradigms and paradigm shifts?"[39] Furthermore, if one falls back on a narrative theology, what precisely comes to mind? Erickson asks:

> What is the difference between the traditional propositional theology and this narrative theology? Indeed, the theology is not really narrative theology, but perhaps, more correctly, "theology of narrative," for theology is a second-level activity and is in propositional rather than narrative form. Either that, or what Pinnock and Grenz are actually giving us is metatheology, the discussion of the method of theology, rather than theology itself, and it is this that is propositional.[40]

5. Finally, we must ask, are Baptists in a position to make constructive contributions to Christian thinking in the years ahead? On balance, the signs are good. Those who have entered into a critique of modernity—Grenz, McClendon, Murphy, and others—have helped to identify the peculiar sense of dissolution and strain that afflicts our age; and they have rightly warned against the prejudices of modernity and shown why these prejudices no longer have the rhetorical power that they once had. Still their rhetoric borrows heavily upon the modern notion of historical optimism and the tireless affirmation of what is "bold" and "new." The courage to "boldly go where no one has gone before" and to adopt "new paradigms"

38. Derrida, *Writing and Difference*, 146.
39. Erickson, *Evangelical Left*, 57.
40. Ibid., 56.

still preaches, but it is a shopworn and threadbare sentiment. The progress of Baptist theology will most likely be tied to an even more striking alternative to modern thought: one that awakens a renewed search for that "good" and that truth by which a people of God can live and die. It will appeal to that latent sentiment that identifies qualities of life and good and beauty with that which is deep and abiding rather than that which is merely new. It will awaken old sentiments that, in fact, have never left us.

Baptists are in a position to aid the awakening because, in a very real sense, they are products of the modern age, since their beginnings are roughly contemporary with Locke, Hume, and Hobbes. Yet at the same time, Baptists represent a brand saved from the ashes of a rapidly secularizing culture, which is to say a culture that is becoming disoriented and forgetful of its goal. Like the moderns, Baptists affirmed the dignity of the individual; but unlike the heart of the modern age, they found this theme of freedom and human dignity not in Promethian dreams of a powerful new role for humanity, but in the transcendent truths of a house "made not with hands, eternal in the heavens" (1 Cor 5:1). As in the Hebrew prophetic movement's recovery of the covenants, and the Reformation's returning to Scripture, the progress of the gospel among Baptists will come from the recollection of those things that were neglected. That is where their power always lay, not in novelty, but in the contemporary recognition that "the Lord our God made a covenant with us in Horeb. Not with our fathers did the Lord make this covenant, but with us, who are all of us here alive this day" (Deut 5:2, 3 RSV).

5

Three Sources of the Secular Mind (1998)[1]

Everything that lives Lives not alone, nor for itself.

—WILLIAM BLAKE

ALLEN TATE DEFINED SECULARISM as the state of a culture in which means have replaced ends.[2] Such a definition is worth exploring, I think, at length. In every area of life, not least of all in academia, one hears the complaint that time is wasted in speculation and the theoretical contemplation of the world when, as Marx said, "the point is to change it." Even in seminaries, where ministers are trained for the more or less specific purpose of helping people to think about life in view of the end—the purpose or goal of life— there is heard the cry that studies should become ever more "practical." I even witnessed an impassioned plea from a trustee that ministers should take a course on reading a balance sheet.

That the practical task should not be abandoned or neglected is clear. What is less clear, however, is that our world—perhaps especially in North America—suffers from a loss of pragmatism and a surfeit of pastors trained in theology, lawyers trained in the philosophy of law, teachers well equipped to think of the ethics of their tasks, and church members whose minds soar in contemplation of the eternal mysteries of the God they profess to believe in. I am afraid that just the reverse is true. We have gradually lost the vocabulary and syntax necessary for speaking meaningfully, even to our own

---

1. Originally published in *Journal of the Evangelical Theological Society* 41, no. 2 (June 1998): 313–21.

2. Tate, *Essays of Four Decades*, 6.

children, about nonmaterial values, nonpragmatic affections, and aims in life that exceed life itself. We speak instead of means, not ends. Why?

A brief review of three trends that have enjoyed a long pilgrimage in the west reveals a common core of sentiment, one that illuminates the habit that Tate refers to: the growing resistance to talk about ends and the replacement of that talk with discussion of means. The first trend is philosophical, the second is moral, and the third is theological. Laying these side by side, we find that it becomes a simple matter at the end to disclose what is the common core and the common motivation among them all.

Three Movements against Transcendence

How should we speak of these trends, which in many ways will appear abstract and therefore irrelevant to the opinion makers of our day? One might begin with three well-known, and often commented upon, results of the trends. As they stand, they will sound familiar and even self-evident to almost everyone. But few recognize the inner core of intimately connected thought or sentiment. On the surface they appear, indeed, to be three entirely different ways of explaining what has happened in secular thought. In fact, as I believe I can show, they are three ways of viewing the same essential movement in modern thought, even though each one concentrates on a distinct result of the movement. The three results of a secular culture, or rather one that has refused to think about its ends, are (1) the loss of authority, (2) the hatred of distinction, and (3) the love of power.

These three results actually give us a good summary of the kind of destructive winds that blow through a culture that has rejected its vision of transcendent ends. What I say here will only be a brief overview. For any one of these approaches to the question, the works that I cite will yield a much more complete treatment of the question involved. My purpose here, however, is not to explore each trend thoroughly but to show that on every side we are dealing with the same problems and the same questions—and they are questions to which the Christian hope gives an enormously satisfying answer. It is an answer that meets the human need not only in terms of intellect but also in terms of the affections: what we love and what we value. Yet because it is an answer that requires surrendering to the facts of human finitude and moral liability, the modern spirit has typically rebelled in these three predictable ways: against authority, against the limits of self (distinction), and against the limits of will.

Three Sources of the Secular Mind (1998)

The Decline of Logical Realism

Richard Weaver made perhaps the liveliest and most far-reaching case for seeing the cultural decline of the west as being strongly tied to the nominalist-realist controversy of the late fourteenth century. He proposed that the widening circles of disorder in Western life can be traced back to a philosophical choice to abandon the idea that universals have a reality that is independent of and higher than the particular existence of things. "Have we forgotten our encounter with the witches on the Heath?" he asks. It was there—in that medieval controversy—that the evil choice was made: "What the witches said to the protagonist of this drama was that man could realize himself more fully if he would only abandon his belief in the existence of transcendentals."[3]

The realists in this controversy—followers of Duns Scotus, for instance—held to ideas that general and abstract categories of things are real, whereas particular things are examples that manifest reality. For example, the idea of a tree and the reality of a particular pine tree do not exist on the same level. Particulars come and go. They are only the temporal manifestation of something that is lasting and does not come into existence and disappear from existence.

The emerging nominalist position, however, insisted that the idea of a tree rises from the particular and concrete existence of trees, to which we assign names. The nominalist assertion, notwithstanding its common designation, runs deeper than the phenomenon of language. It is not simply the idea of giving names to things that is implied. It is that the concept of the world, the vision of the world—including categories, names, principles, virtues, and the like—are generated by the human imagination or reason and projected upon a reality that only consists of the concrete and particular things.

I must admit, however, that to state this controversy in such stark contrasts is not entirely fair. There was not a single nominalist position. There were a number of nominalist systems that ranged along a scale from moderate to radical. And though nominalism stated in such stark terms may sound like a preamble to materialism, it certainly was not the case in the minds of its earliest proponents. William of Occam in England and Gabriel Biel in Germany were leading intellectuals in this revolution in worldview. But they were also leading Christian thinkers who believed deeply in

---

3. Weaver, *Ideas Have Consequences*, 2–3.

a transcendent reality. It was a long time before the full implications of a nominalist position would appear in discussions among intellectuals, and even longer before the impact of such thought weighed heavily in ordinary public life and discourse.

But it was, as Weaver points out, the first faint shadow of something ominous that was to bring about a change in the western concept of reality. The issue that comes to light, however, is of huge importance in the ordering of human life. The issue is no less than "whether there is a source of truth higher than, and independent of, man." As Weaver pointed out: "The practical result of nominalist philosophy is to banish the reality which is perceived by the intellect and to posit as reality that which is perceived by the senses." Thus "the question of what the world was made for now becomes meaningless because the asking of it presupposes something prior to nature in the order of existents."[4]

Among the results of this intellectual change stands one of central importance. The articulation of values implies an abstract ordering of things. One action is seen as more virtuous than another. One thing is more valuable than another. One mode of art is sublime, another is worthless and ugly. One boy knows his mathematics, another needs improvement, a third has failed. The sluggard is foolish, the industrious is wise. We cannot speak of human action, social order, justice, beauty, virtue without implying a hierarchy. The moment we attempt to pretend that everything is on the same level and that evaluation is impossible we find ourselves caught up in every possible contradiction. Because the truth is that we do imply that one action is preferable to another, and one thing is of greater value than another, whether we wish to do so or not. Otherwise all things and all actions are meaningless, and the most sensible thing is to lapse into silence.

But the point raised by the trend toward nominalism is whether in fact these hierarchies of value have any intrinsic meaning, or whether they are actually arbitrary constructions of the human will. Are these generalities and abstractions of value rooted in a reality apart from the world of particulars, or are they simply projected upon the world as human conventions? It is the tendency of nominalism to convince us that such evaluations are arbitrary and are imposed upon a world of undifferentiated particulars.

The moral confusion this state of mind could cause is obvious. (It is with some indebtedness to the human being's stubborn attachment to reality that the full implications of this thinking seldom appear.) For example,

---

4. Ibid., 3–4.

Three Sources of the Secular Mind (1998)

several years ago I was involved in a panel discussion on the subject of ethics and the environmental crisis. The speaker before me on the program tried to base his argument against human exploitation of nature on the notion that, as he said, "human beings have no more right to live than bears." This is a popular and very modern theme, and I imagine that the audience and the media responded to it favorably.

But I thought that it was also a seriously wrongheaded approach to saving the environment. Granted, bears have value—and one that even transcends their value to humanity. As I tried to show however, if everything is of equal value, then there is no hierarchy of values to appeal to when one is trying to save the bear. And if one thing in nature is not inherently more important than another, then the survival of one species or another, and the question of whether bears are not of more service as bear rugs, becomes a question that can only be resolved on the level of power and conflict.

The Love of Power

A second attempt at ordering life without transcendence is by appeal to power. There is something present in modern thought, as Jürgen Moltmann has pointed out, that identifies God with simple, direct, coercive power. And in the same way that theologians identify God with power, the world at large has been drawn to a worship of power.

This "apotheosis of power," as I have called it, has brought on what Moltmann calls the "crisis of domination." In terms of the ecological crisis he says that human beings have learned that their proper relationship to nature is one of domination and exploitation.

Where did this originate? Some would say it comes from the Bible, where the Genesis creation story tells us that man was given domination over all that God has placed on earth. Moltmann denies that this is the source. In the first place, the idea of dominion in the OT involves the idea of protection as well as ordering, and it was only at a much later date that the role of humanity was seen as that of exploiter, as one who uses power for the purpose of domination and to serve selfish ends.[5]

---

5. Genesis 2:15, Moltmann points out, "talks about 'the Garden of Eden' which human beings are 'to till and keep/ So human mastery over the earth is intended to resemble the cultivating and protective work of a gardener. Nothing is said about predatory exploitation" (*God in Creation*, 30).

Safeguarding a Truly Catholic Vision of the World

Instead, Moltmann says, we see this notion arising about four hundred years ago. With the coming of greater and greater possibilities within the realm of science and technology, he explains, there was also a tendency to see God's preeminent attribute as *potentia absoluta*—absolute power. He continues, "Power became the foremost predicate of deity, not goodness and truth. But how can the human being acquire power, so that he may resemble his God? Through science and technology; for 'knowledge is power,' as Francis Bacon exultantly proclaimed."[6]

Of enormous influence in the emerging experience of science was the thinking of René Descartes. He states that the aim of science is to make men "masters and possessors of nature."[7] Thus nature becomes an object to be analyzed—not to be contemplated for its own sake but to determine how it might yield to human purposes and designs. The object of science comes to be to divide and conquer. Thus human beings come to live not as members of a created order in community with nature, though in a unique role. Instead they come as its lord and owner. Science becomes the instrument by which this relationship is made possible—if not in fact, at least to the imagination. For that reason the vision that has dominated so much of the past four centuries, encouraged by undeniably spectacular gains in science and technology, has been one of man dominating nature.

The scientific ideal, along with its attendant notion that knowledge is power, is not confined of course to the natural sciences. Auguste Comte envisioned the potential of science as a basis for a new society. Karl Marx envisioned scientific socialism. Sigmund Freud wished his psychoanalysis to be seen as a science, with some effective power in the realm of the psyche. War has increasingly become a contest of technologies. Businesses, bureaucracies and churches depend upon the analysis of society, made believable by reams of computerized data—all giving the impression (whether or not it is more or less illusory) that the possessors of such knowledge stand in a power relationship to the populations they wish to influence.

The difficulty with such a relationship and such a vision is that it implies the exertion of the will over something or someone. That thing—so moved by the will—becomes no longer a subject with which one enjoys companionable mutual relationship. It becomes an object. And the more perfectly an object obeys the will, the more it becomes a mere extension

---

6. Ibid., 27.
7. Descartes, *Discours de la Methode*, 634 (cited by Moltmann, *God in Creation*, 27).

of the self. Relationship requires otherness. Power overcomes otherness; it eliminates relationship.

Students of the NT will recall that Jesus is remembered as one who resisted the use of power to accomplish his purpose. That offer to exercise power—as Messiah or King—was seen as the peculiarly satanic temptation (cf. Matt 4:8–10; 16:21–23).

It is in the NT more than anywhere else that we see power as in the first instance a destroyer. Service, suffering and love imply respecting the subject, the otherness, the Thou (as Martin Buber expressed it) in the ones to whom we relate.

Thus Paul described the husband's role as "head of the wife" precisely as "Christ is head of the church." This means that he sacrifices self-interest for her in imitation of Christ, who "loved the church and gave himself for it" (Eph 5:25). And Jesus told his disciples not to follow the example of the Gentiles whose princes "exercise dominion over them, and . . . excessive authority upon them" (Matt 21:25). Instead, if any would be great, that one must be a servant of the rest. That was in Jesus' teaching the nature of the kingdom. It was in fact the nature of life itself—because power, though necessary within limits, has this inevitable quality about it: It destroys.

A pediatrician whom I know is widely appreciated for his lectures on childrearing. The parent, he points out, has two important assets from the very beginning of the child's life: (1) Obviously the parent is bigger and stronger than the child, so the mother or father can and must force the child to do the parent's will. (2) The child wants the parent, and this asset is easily transformed into wanting to please the parent. The doctor goes on to explain that the object of childrearing is to bring children to the point where they go the right way as a result of their own free will. Often—and if things go well, less and less often—the parent resorts to the use of his size and might in order to force the child to go the right way.

However—and here is a major point of parental wisdom—the parent must recognize that to employ force is always done at the expense of the second asset. The child's natural attraction to the parent is diminished to the extent that the parent must use force. It creates a barrier of resentment: It is perhaps only temporary, but it is there. So the point the doctor makes is this: Use this remedy when necessary, but remember that it is expensive medicine. Power always diminishes relationships. This lesson applies to all areas of life: Domination destroys, love makes alive. In a fallen world, one cannot exist without the other. Love is given a space in which to grow only where law, domination and force impose a certain order. But power must always be seen as the means (and a costly means at that) and not as an end.

The Hatred of Distinction

A third fashion in modern thought is theological in nature, and it is one that in a way summarizes the other two and has an enormous bearing on modern life. It is properly called pantheism. If nominalism promised relief from metaphysical absolutes, and if power provides freedom from circumstances that frustrate the will, then pantheism combines the promise of toppling absolutes and dissolving individual limits.

To the popular mind, pantheism relates to eastern religions and to the Western adoption of Vedanta Hinduism. Pantheism simply means, however, an identification of the world with God: The "all" of the world is God, and God is all. A case can be made that philosophical pantheism has played as large a role in Western thought as it ever did in the East. While Hinduism is often described as pantheistic, one will seldom find that form of philosophical Hinduism in practice in Indian communities.

In the West, by contrast, beginning with pre-Socratic Greek philosophy one can find in pantheism a constant possibility among the range of philosophical and theological options. And in many instances it has been among the strongest intellectual influences in society. Such was the case, for instance, during the several centuries (from about the third century BC until the rise of Christianity) that the stoic philosophy filled the vacuum left by religious cynicism and skepticism in the Greco-Roman world. As Robert Pattison has pointed out, "pantheism is as old as philosophy, and every age has had its believers."[8] From El Hallaj of the Islamic Sufis to William Blake in the Christian tradition, from every religious camp there has emerged the possibility of a pantheistic vision of reality.[9]

---

8. In a book on rock music, *Triumph of Vulgarity*, Pattison points out that the popular expression of pantheism is manifest as a preference for vulgarity—that is, things that are common and unrefined by attention to forms, convention, morals and manners.

9. Kraus pointed this out when he commented on the ubiquity of pantheism: "Pantheism confirms itself as an authentic natural product of the human mind by the fact that it has arisen on the Ganges as on the Rhine, and in the age of Xenophanes as in that of Spinoza, and among Brahmins, Cabalists and mystics, theologians and philosophers—in short, everywhere and always, and in all kinds of intellects" ("Über den Pantheismus," *Vermischte Schriften*). Like the other two developments I mentioned, pantheism does not necessarily spread outward from a philosophy or religion so much as it represents

Three Sources of the Secular Mind (1998)

Aristotle assumed that Xenophanes' (c. 570–480 BC) idea of God included his quality of being coextensive with the universe—what we would call pan-theism. Mellissus of Samos (c. 450) was certainly a pantheistic philosopher, as was Heraclitus (c. 536–470), who thought that all opposites are absorbed into a cosmic whole. "Things taken together are whole and not whole . . . Out of all there comes a unity, and out of unity all things."[10] Naturally, then, the theological conclusion is that "God is day night, winter summer, war peace, satiety hunger." He is the dissolution of opposites, the end of distinction, the abolition of limits.[11]

It seems that pantheism is not a particular religious system of belief. Rather, it is a theoretical tendency whenever a religion begins to reach out beyond the grossly material, the particular, and the provincial expression to one of universal and therefore more abstract concepts. Thus Hinduism, the religion of the Indus Valley, became pantheistic only at that stage when it emerged from its mythic expression to the more theoretical attempts at universal wisdom in the Upanishads and in Vedanta ("end of the Vedas") Hinduism in the first century BC. Stoicism, a Western pantheism, gradually replaced the declining polytheistic Greco-Roman religions under the reforming influence of philosophy. It seems that whenever there is an attempt to reconcile the world of multiple things with the unity and oneness of the world, there is the option of short-circuiting that difficulty by declaring the multiplicity as *maya* (illusion). The temptation to resolve the question in this manner, however, is no more eastern than it is western, and it has made its appearance in every society of advanced culture with a highly developed need for abstract thought.

The only reason such a tendency feels alien in the west is that theism—in the form of Christianity, Judaism and Islam—has so long resisted the pantheistic alternative. For several reasons, theists have detected a grave threat to their understanding of God and their understanding of human life in the pantheistic alternative. They have accurately sensed that a faith that relies upon the kind of discipline (in moral and devotional life) that calls for self-giving love cannot long endure where distinctions are seen ultimately as illusions.

---

a central tendency in the human heart and mind that is so universal that its expression is inevitably found from time to time and necessarily feeds that hunger for asserting the self-will over the environment.

10. Cited in Kirk and Raven, *Presocratic Philosophies*, 191.

11. Ibid., 192.

Safeguarding a Truly Catholic Vision of the World

The Pain of Life and the "Happiness" of Death

In these three modern trends—the rejection of absolutes in nominalism, the pursuit of power in science, and the loss of distinction in pantheism—we have three trends that are, in effect, aspects of the same trend. Each of these trends appeals, in a certain way, to what I will call the imperialistic self. They respond to a metaphysical threat, one that every human being suffers in one way or another. This threat is directed against the self. It says in effect, "You are limited, you are finite." You are limited, first of all, by the otherness of existence—by other persons, other things. These are not simply extensions of your own self-consciousness, but they exist apart from you and without regard to you. Moreover the fact of death is the final irrefutable statement of human finitude. It is its ultimate expression and the final insult to the self that imagines itself the center from which all reality radiates.

An aspect of that metaphysical insult is that the individual and his society must respond to an outside reality. The world will not yield to the vagrant wishes and vain desires of the human being. The development since the Renaissance in rejecting realism (by the rise of nominalism) has increasingly allowed us to believe there are no absolutes. It has promoted the notion that society yields to the unfettered imagination, that only freedom is absolute.

Thus the assurance (via nominalism) that there are no transcendentals, no universals, no absolutes, comes as a relief. The imperialistic self imagines it is free from moral contradictions and thus from guilt. Science likewise can be imagined as the source of unlimited domination in the physical realm. And pantheism takes away the fear of God, for if the boundary between me and God has been repealed, then who is to say whether I have been taken up into God, or God has been taken up into me?

Thus theology becomes psychology. Talk of ultimate ends becomes meaningless, for the horizon beyond the limited self has disappeared. We can only speak of operations, of practice, of techniques. As the Cheshire cat advised Alice in Lewis Carroll's fantasy, if you do not know where you are going, then the direction really does not matter. Under such circumstances, secularism has become complete. The world must discover all over again how to speak about ends. And once again the gospel becomes required reading.

6

Simms's *Sabbath Lyrics* and the Reclaiming of Sacred Time in the Religious Imagination[1] (2000)

Simms's *Sabbath Lyrics: or, Songs from Scripture* might best be understood against the background of his social criticism of the 1840s. The prevailing theme—one which proved itself prophetic in light of the ensuing sectional conflict a decade or so later—underscored the remarkable difference between a society whose aim is a settled and harmonious life, and one whose aim is pressing toward the limits of industry and dynamism. The metaphors of "rest," "peace," "shalom," are appropriate to the former, while the latter exalts "power," "conquest," and "profit." Simms could see the loss in modernity, and especially in America, of the virtues implied, for instance in "The Peace of Christ's Empire" (his song on Isa 11), as a profound capitulation to the temptations of market and materialism—a temptation at work in both the South and North, but in differing measures. His thesis might be paraphrased, "A restless society is a more or less barbarous society, and a more or less violent society." In these verses we see an attempt to restore the public value of biblical rest, so as to rescue the true meaning of human labor.

A thesis is not the first thing that will strike the reader of these verses with the subtitle *Christmas Gift of Love*. They appear at first sight to be a casual collection of verses, prompted for the most part by readings from

---

1. A version of this essay was presented at the Simms 2000 Symposium in Charleston, South Carolina, in January 2000. Originally published in *Simms Review* 8, no. 1 (2000): 15–26.

Scripture, most of which—but not all of which—reflect upon Advent themes. Along with these that are obviously and explicitly drawn from Scripture are a number with no Scripture reference and which address topics as varied as an infant's death or an early death (to which he devotes five songs), the fact of death itself, the waning of the evening light, worship in the natural temple of the forest, hope in God, the fallen warrior, prayer for a fevered child, martyrdom, the quest for peace, duty, despondency, and the birth of the true Shepherd. I will not insist that Simms had a theme which he consciously wished to articulate in his collection. If the thesis is accidental instead of intentional, it nevertheless reveals something of the poet and something of his intentions in publishing this collection. There were marked philosophical preoccupations that Simms exhibited during the 1840s and it would be something of a wonder indeed if he divested himself of these very strong intellectual predispositions just for the sake of producing a collection of pious verses for the season.

In order to detect this thesis we will first examine the title itself and its implications, then the arrangement of the songs from Scripture, and finally the recurring emphases from the lyrics themselves. Next we will look at this quietly emerging thesis in light of his social criticism from the 1840s. And last, we will examine Simms's achievement here in the context of the philosophical vexation that marked all of modernity and which casts its shadow upon the struggles of a new American nation at the time of its greatest crisis.

Detecting the Thesis Dimly

The title *Sabbath Verses* might itself provide a clue as to what Simms had in mind with this collection. Sabbath is the Lord's Day, a day of worship, devotion to religious practice, and rest. In using this title, Simms appeared to have an interest in the juxtaposition of rest and work, the tension between a dynamistic view of life and a harmonious view of life, and the contrast between the restlessness of barbarity and the settled and pacific habits of civilization. That being the case, there is reason to suspect that Simms had an interest in the kinds of theological discussions brought to bear on the meaning of "Sabbath" in Scripture.

In mid-nineteenth-century Charleston, theological symbols retained a depth of meaning that was later lost in the sentimental vacuity of the mid-twentieth century. The Christian doctrine most influential in these parts

Simms's Sabbath Lyrics *and the Reclaiming of Sacred Time*

was Calvinism, especially as that was mediated through the Westminster Confession, the *Book of Common Prayer*, and as it was moderated philosophically by the Scottish Common Sense school of thought. For Calvin, the Sabbath was no mere day of religious observance, but a "fore shadowing of spiritual rest."[2] It represents the goal of creation and the goal of existence and is therefore a symbol not confined to one day but operates as a sign of permanence in the midst of flux. The Sabbath represents the "very substance of truth" and therefore "is not confined within a single day but extends through the whole course of our life, until, completely dead to ourselves, as one filled with the life of God."[3] It is therefore an eschatological sign of the world to come. "The Sabbath points forward to the Sabbath in another world, a world which is entirely Sabbath," wrote Israel Abrahams, a contemporary of Simms and a Reader in Talmudic and Rabbinic Literature in Cambridge.[4]

For the reflective members of a Christian or Jewish society, the Sabbath represents that which is permanent in the midst of time—the eternal within time. A. J. Herschel referred to it as a "temple within time."[5]

That Simms had all of this in mind when he titled his collection is rather doubtful. I will only insist that he meant by it more than the sentimental evoking of something vaguely religious. For after all, he lived in a neighborhood not unaccustomed to theology in the more rigorous sense. Charleston is the city that bore the legacy of Richard Furman, whose sermons would be considered far too demanding for contemporary ears. Simms lived mere blocks from James Petigru Boyce, a disciple of Charles Hodge, and in his own right a theologian of national stature. These were the days, in South Carolina, of James Henley Thornwell, and in the South of R. L. Dabney. It is tempting to read back twentieth-century popular religion—that is, religion with theology largely strained out—into mid-nineteenth-century discourse; but it is not wise. Whether or not Simms himself thought in terms of permanence over against flux when he approached the text of the Bible can only be established by looking beyond the title to the text itself.

---

2. *Institutes of the Christian Religion*, 2.8.28.
3. *Institutes*, 2.8.30.
4. Abrahams, "Sabbath (Jewish)," 891.
5. Heschel, *The Sabbath*.

Safeguarding a Truly Catholic Vision of the World

The Arrangement of the Collection

The arrangement of Simms's pieces in *Sabbath Lyrics* strikes one as significant. Although it is impossible to retrieve precisely what he had in mind with this arrangement, it can be said with certainty that it is neither a random selection nor what one might expect from scripture passages sequenced according to the Advent readings. Yet there appears to be an order. I want to suggest an ordering by giving conjectural titles to the parts. (Please see the accompanying chart.) There is no claim of infallibility here: I want only to suggest that in the sequential grouping of the poetic pieces we find something of the thoughts or the intellectual problems that engaged Simms during the 1840s, leading up to the 1849 publication of *Sabbath Lyrics*.

It is tempting to raise the mere biographical point that is the explicit subject of several of these pieces. Of the fourteen children born to Chevillette, only five survived their father. From 1837 until the publication of *Sabbath Lyrics*, seven had been born—six daughters, and one son. In that same period, four of the daughters died: one was only a few days old, two were around one year old, and one was nearly three.

Yet the poetic imagination of Simms is engaged with more than the fact of loss and grief, as significant as this must have been for him. Rather he reflects upon the more general experience of life which these episodes of birth and death make both vivid and pathetic. He reflects upon the larger theme of the ravages of time, and he seeks after that within time that offers solace and safety from the general dissolution that accompanies the passage of things and events. He seeks for what is permanent, or at least, lasting. In this light, death does not merely represent itself, but it represents for the Christian thinker "the last enemy" (in the Apostle Paul's language) and that which most deeply marks time as unredeemed. The Greek god Chronos, from which we take the word chronological, is also called the destroyer. If time means only eventual destruction and loss, it can only gain purposefulness by that which escapes the ravages of time.

In the ancient and medieval mind, the contrary of this inexorable ruin to which all things run in time is the notion of "rest," which means that time runs toward a goal or purpose—an eschatological goal, a telos—that is secure against the ravages of Chronos. Thus St. Augustine could say, "We were made for Thee, O God, and our hearts are restless until we find rest in Thee."[6] Rest in this sense is not idleness, but, as Thomas Merton said, "the

---

6. A more traditional rendering of the passage in *Confessions*, book 1, chapter 1, and also found in Augustine, *Confessions*, 21.

highest form of activity." Nor is it the obliteration of death. That is why the Christian prayer, "Rest in peace," is not a concession to death but, in fact, an *invocation against death.*

In this poetry that includes many explicit references to destruction, loss, desolation, grief, and death, we also find the poetic grasp of that which promises hope, redemption, and rest. The birth of Jesus is then seen in greatest relief against the destruction of Jerusalem, the judgment of Moab, the desolation of exile, and the death of children.

At the opening we find the theme unveiled: the ambiguity of all life in "The Sacred Minstrel," the identification of the "temple" with the "father's house" in "The Church at Christmas," and the four-lined epitaph "For an Infant's Grave." This opening is followed by contemplation on those things that last: "the Peace of Christ's Empire," "Christ the Conqueror," "The Bread of Life," that is distinct from commerce and "Brotherly Union." In the midst of this is a contemplation of "The Rejection of Christ" and the division within the church: the offer of permanent things and their rejection. Contrasting with this offer of peace (or "rest") is the note of judgment in the next three pieces, devoted to prophecies from Isaiah about Moab and Israel (Ephraim) who have rejected peace and been rewarded with ruin.

Next Simms shifts to the subject, not of permanent things, nor of destruction, but of how these two are actually mingled in life, how the promise and hope exist along with exile, destruction, and ruin. The topic dominates the next six poems.

But the truth of what is permanent is not always apparent. Thus people will cling to false hopes, as Simms shows in the next four pieces, ending this section with "False Prophets."

A distinction is made in the next group of poems, culminating in "The Birth of Christ." Christ is the incarnation (in time) of that which is not ravaged by time. "A chief whose birth has been of old / Even from eternity."

How then do we live in exile, where hope and despair dwell together? That is the subject of the next section, beginning with "Prayer for the Exile" and ending with "The Cry of the Drowning."

Joy is possible even in exile. That is the point of the next section, beginning fittingly with "Song of Solomon."

Finally he takes the question of the movement from despondency to peace, touching heavily upon the death of children and moving to the birth of the divine child who becomes the "true shepherd." Along the way he affirms, along with Ps 127, that children are a gift from heaven. Such a statement, for Simms, transcends disappointment, grief, and the deadliness of time's ultimate effect.

Sabbath Lyrics in the Light of Simms's Social Criticism of the 1840s

Simms's preoccupation with permanence over against flux in these poems is seen in its strongest light when viewed along side his social criticism of the same period. Two sources of Simms's thought from this period come to us in the form of orations. One, delivered in 1842 at the University of Alabama, was published in 1843. It is entitled *The Social Principle: The True Source of National Permanence*. The other was delivered at Oglethorpe University and published in 1847 under the title *Self-Development*. These are remarkable orations, filled with revelations of his social philosophy and causing his poetry to become luminous at points that it might otherwise appear to be either obscure or commonplace.

In these writings, three themes can be seen as sub-themes of Simms's more abstract concern with the search for permanence in the midst of flux, and purpose in the midst of randomness. They are (1) domesticity and civilization, (2) the sirens of money and commerce, and (3) the idea of vocation or purpose in life.

(1) *Domesticity and civilization*. The reason the English prevailed over the French and the Spanish in settling the New World, Simms argues, is that the English intended, more than the other two, to live here. They built their homes and cottages, planted their trees, and invested in the generations to come. This is the domestic principle which is, according to Simms, the "true source of national permanence." "The progress of one man, thus endowing his little cottage with love and comfort, provokes the emulation of his neighbor, and thus hamlets rise, and great cities, even in a wilderness like this!"[7] The pleasures of home constitutes "the order which regulates without being seen—the authority which is felt without being heard."[8]

Over against this development of settled and civil life, the fact of war, including the Revolutionary War, "threw us back in this respect." In addition, the mobility and transitory habits of a people decrease their power to develop civilizing institutions. Simms writes, "In degree, all wanderers

---

7. Simms, *Social Principle*, 15.
8. Ibid., 19.

cease to be laborers. Their habits become desultory and unsettled. They obey impulses rather than laws, and toil in obedience to their humours rather than their necessities."[9] "A wandering people," he concludes, "is more or less a barbarous one."[10]

In *Sabbath Lyrics* we see again how important is this domestic principle. Simms speaks of the home more than the church, or one might say instead of the church. In "The Church at Christmas," he speaks not of the church, but

> God's temple is a father's home,
> Where love and mercy still have sway;
> Thither his happy children come,
> With festive wreath and cheerful lay.

Domestic tranquility is the source of strength, as he shows in "The Fear of God the Security for Peace" based on Ps 128. Moab, on the other hand, like all barbarian peoples, is undone by its grasping restlessness. Thus it is fitting, reflecting on Isa 15, that

> Her maids, at fords of Arnon,
> Like birds that find no rest,
> Grow weary still of seeking[11]

(2) *The Sirens of money and commerce.* In *The Social Principle*, Simms complains that Americans, South as well as North, have gotten into the fatal habit of reducing social goals to money and social life to that of commerce. This has a similar effect upon a people that mobility and rootlessness have. It works against the cultivation of institutions that sustain a life of refinement and order. A people whose life is reduced to commerce, no less than a wondering people, is more or less a barbarian people. He finds the example in the Southern planter who devoted himself to "the production of one commodity only which could find a market." Thus, the "whole labor of the planter was expended,—not in the cultivation of the soil,—for the proper cultivation of a soil improves it,—but in extorting by violence from its bosom, seed and stalk, alike, of the wealth which it contained. He slew the goose that he might grasp, at one moment its whole golden treasure."[12]

9. Ibid., 37.
10. Ibid., 36.
11. Simms, *Sabbath Lyrics*, 17.
12. Simms, *Social Principle*, 42.

The results follow. The farm family easily abandons the land for other land that will yield crops more easily. And there is little to prevent this moving about and this rootlessness. Simms writes:

> He laid out no gardens, the graveled walks and tropical beauties of which would have fastened, as with the spells of Armida, his reluctant footsteps—planted no favorite trees, whose mellowing shade, covering the graves of father, mother or favorite child—would have seemed too sacred for desertion—would have seemed like venerated relatives whom it would be cruel to abandon in their declining years. These, are the substantial marks of a civilization, by which we distinguish an improving people.[13]

(3) *The idea of vocation.* Such preoccupation with commerce has its effects in the artistic realm as well, which is the principle issue of *Self-Development* (1847). The proper object of ambition is to follow in obedience to one's vocation, since "he cannot be a Christian, who fails in obedience to the laws of his own nature—who suffers his faculties to sleep in sloth, and stifles his peculiar endowment, which is his *one* talent, in the folds of a napkin!"[14] Yet the interests of the market and the interests of a person's "peculiar endowment" are often quite distinct, causing the ambitious soul to be distracted from his or her intended vocation in order to answer the less substantial voices of vulgar commerce and its "miserable catalogue of vanities." "And for such as these," Simms emphasizes, "what years are sacrificed, what gifts squandered, what noble natures wrecked forever!" Thus "money ... through the most silly appetites, becomes the master passion of mankind. It chains the virtues—bends the moods—buys the affections—tames Ambition—subjugates Love, and walks, the Universal Conqueror!"[15]

Again in *Sabbath Lyrics* we find these same emphases. "The Bread of Life" is based on Matt 4 and bears the epigraph "Man shall not live by bread alone, but by every word that proceedeth out of the mouth of God."

> Ah! Still in vain, the human care,
> That ever craves the morrow's food,
> And seeks provision, far and near,
> For moral want and passing mood;
> That wastes the soil, that robs the mine

---

13. Ibid., 43.
14. Simms, *Self-Development*, 40.
15. Ibid., 38.

Simms's Sabbath Lyrics *and the Reclaiming of Sacred Time*

In sleepless march that nought supplies;

Institutional religion itself is apt to be swept along in the commercial trivialization of things. This is perhaps why Simms, while he shows great devotion to the Christian tradition, tends to show little respect for the church as an institution. His scenes of worship are likely to be those of a shrine provided by nature or the home itself. In "Forest Worship" he speaks of this tension between true religion and its commercial imitation:

Ah! Vain is that worship, whose vision
Still craves for the gold on the shrine . . .[16]

Civilization, the Idea of 'Rest,' and the Restlessness of Modernity

The over-arching concern, I would argue, both in *Sabbath Lyrics* and in the social criticism of the period in Simms's thought—which in fact has a significant bearing upon his later experience and thought during the war and afterward—might be stated briefly. The life of a community, if it is to afford those forms of experience for which the human being is made, must with some degree of success discover and cultivate permanence in the midst of the inevitable flux, restlessness, and change of human existence.

In his religious poetry especially, Simms does not underestimate the serious difficulty of this prerequisite to all civilizing habits and institutions. Death itself is the ultimate affront to the hopeful striving after permanence. Death mocks the efforts and the active life of community, tempting the faint-hearted to believe that nothing in fact except death is permanent.

The soul, too, has its night, a perilous hour,—
The mind its madness, and the heart its pain;[17]

Thus in "Despondency and Yearning," he pits the mocking-power of death over against the longing for that which transcends death and is more powerful than death:

He may not rest with idiot satisfaction,
Beneath the cank'ring chain, the curse, the clay,
But, longing for a wing of sleepless action,

16. Simms, *Sabbath Lyrics*, 53.
17. Ibid., 70.

Safeguarding a Truly Catholic Vision of the World

> Soar for the blessed clime, the enduring day.[18]

It is in the facing of death—which is, as I have said earlier, the ultimate expression of flux—that the hard won proof of something sable, dependable, that still, unchanging center of things that resists the ravages of time and thus resists death, reveals itself. That which is truly permanent value cannot be found easily, not in those "toys" for which we normally strive:

> How small its worth, how brief its measure,
> How formed to cheat, how little to endure.[19]

In this "there is nought sure but sorrow and transition."[20] But it is in facing this reality that the true *telos* of life comes to light, because

> Man, only, has the privilege to wear
> His crown of thorns—far nobler than the laurel,—
> And wins his immortality from care[21]

Thus how fitting it is when

> 'Twas in the year when King Uzziah died,
> That, in a vision,—seated in his pride,
> These eyes behold Jehovah on his throne,
> High lifted, and in majesty, alone.[22]

The sentiments expressed by these verses, and the philosophy that makes them more explicit in his public orations, are hardly in keeping with the prevailing dogma of the modern West. It is a countervailing sentiment: one which expresses the skepticism regarding all those intellectual predispositions that we usually associate with the European Enlightenment: historical optimism, individualism, autonomous reason, anti-traditionalism—marks of modernity that characterize both his world and ours. More to the point, Simms here rejects a fundamental modern prejudice, one that began, more or less, with Thomas Hobbes, and marks—more than anything else—the true spirit of modernity. Simms uses terms such as permanence, purpose, "rest," stability, eternity, and "place" as the fundaments of

---

18. Ibid.
19. Ibid., 64.
20. Ibid.
21. Ibid.
22. Ibid., 59.

civilization. This contradicts the modern preference for movement, change, dynamism, utopianism, progress, and revolution, as indicators of health and prosperity.

Between the two is a preference for metaphors. For the ancients the natural state of things is "rest." For the moderns, "motion." For one, there is a given purpose for things which is the object of their motion. For the other there is no given purpose, only motion and dynamism, which might be brought to bear upon the purposes which human beings shall determine on their own, by their will and their imagination. Between these two metaphors is an abyss, one that separates two worlds, worlds utterly different and that bear the possibility of quite different cultures, and that produce in time different sorts of human beings. For the very notion of humanity and the human being's knowledge of things expressed by Thomas Traherne and René Descartes, for instance, are *very* different. For Traherne, "that any thing may be found to be an infinit Treasure, its Place must be found in Eternity, and in Gods Esteem. For as there is a Time, so there is a Place for all Things. Evry thing in its Place is Admirable Deep and Glorious: out of its Place like a Wandering Bird, is Desolat and Good for Nothing."[23] A very different idea of human knowledge is found when Descartes declares that the aim of science is to make men "maîtres et possesseurs de la nature."[24]

What has happened in modern thought, however, is that we have attempted to do without the notion of a goal as something that is given point of reference,[25] what Aristotle would call a "final cause." The idea of a final cause has faded away. The world is explained in material causes (that out of which something is made) and efficient causes (that by which something is made), but not final cause (that for the sake of which something is

---

23. Also there is a remarkable piece by Augustine on the "weight of live": "A body tends by its weight towards the place proper to it—weight does not necessarily ten towards the lowest place but towards its proper place. Oil poured over water is borne on the surface of the water, water poured over oil sinks below the oil: it is by their weight that they are moved and seek their proper place. Things out of their place are in motion: they come to their place and are at rest. My love is my weight: wherever I go my love is what brings me there."

24. Descartes, *Discours de la Méthode*, 634.

25. Modern thinkers such as John Dewey want to express this as a "fixed" point of reference, as if the adequacy of the idea is totally dependent on the adequacy of a certain metaphor. To say that the "good" is fixed and stable is only an attempt to say that it does not depend upon us, but something that stands over against us—it is *given* and perhaps discoverable, but not invented and the product of artifice.

made). Ever since Hobbes, the idea of *final* cause as indeed a *cause* has been doubted, or at least neglected.

This same idea of often articulated in terms of "motion." The biblical idea of "rest" contains within it the assumption that the motion of people and things and events anticipates a time of "rest," that is, a time in which their motion is complete, will find its end. It is a way of conceptualizing that things and people have a purpose. Augustine's famous line about his own restless life in his *Confessions* reflects this strong biblical sentiment. This sort of metaphor makes sense in a world that believes things exist, they are "set in motion," for a purpose. In that world, the language of purposefulness, moral responsibility, and moral choice comes naturally.

Hobbes was elated, however, when he thought he had "discovered" a new principle in his encounter with Galileo. The natural state of things is not "rest" but "motion"—all things are in motion, and this, not rest, marks the nature of the world and all things and people in it. This concept, as Hobbes realized, had profound political implications. If *rest* is not the natural state of things, and motion is, then there are no given purposes toward which the world or we move. The nature of things is not *given* and *discoverable*, or it is not something the true nature of which must be *revealed* to us, as every titular head of Western culture from Aristotle to Thomas Aquinas assumed, but it is subject always to change. And if subject to change, it is malleable; and if malleable then the world is essentially unstable. In that cause, any order that exists, exists because of the action of human beings upon things. Order is a product of the human will. It is something we make, not something we find and participate in. As Thomas Spragens put it in his *The Politics of Motion*, a book on the thought of Thomas Hobbes, "A world of 'restless' motion which has no *telos* contained restless men who had no *summum bonum*."[26]

The most characteristic feature of modern thought is this change in orientation. Hobbes's "discovery" that all things are in motion and that there is no such thing as a state of "rest" toward which all things move is almost laughable in its apparent naïveté. One wonders if Hobbes is faking an inability to comprehend subtlety, or if he is resorting purposefully to a kind of primitive adoption of literal language. In either event, he takes the metaphor of "rest" as a description of physical destiny. But the seriousness of his modern change of orientation is nevertheless real. If things have purpose—that is, they come to rest, have a destiny—then human beings have a

---

26. Spragens, *Politics of Motion*, 205.

theoretical task before them: they must come to *understand* in order to *act*. But if things have no inherent purpose, and there is no "givenness," and no meaning in using the term "Good" besides what we voluntarily ascribe to it, then our attempts to understand might be considered as tactics in the strategy of coping with the world, but the essential thing is not to understand but to act. And this is what is characteristic of modernity: the shift from the intellect (as a means of understanding the world) to the will (as a means of changing the world).

It is this strong modern predisposition that Simms encountered and challenged in his poetry and his criticism. We are tempted to think that the difficulties Simms encountered in the late nineteenth century, and continuing into our own, were merely products of the historical events of a few decades in American history. Perhaps the truth of it is that the deeply rooted resistance that he has encountered was caused by a world that had drunk deeply at the fountain of modernity. And perhaps only now—in the early twenty-first century—when the bitter dregs of modernity are beginning to affect us, and when the boastful claims of the Enlightenment no longer enchant us so, can we fully appreciate the wisdom of the South's greatest man of letters.

Sabbath Lyrics: A Christmas Gift of Love

By William Gilmore Simms

Topic	Title	Scripture
Mixed blessings and woes	The Sacred Minstrel	Isa 30
	The Church at Christmas	Isa 60
	For an Infant's Grave	
Permanent Things	The Peace of Christ's Empire	Isa 11
	Christ the Conqueror	Isa 63
	Promise for Zion	Isa 51
	The Rejection of Christ	Isa 53
	The Bread of Life	Matt 4
	Brotherly Union	Ps 133
Judgment	The Desolation of Moab	Isa 16

Safeguarding a Truly Catholic Vision of the World

Topic	Title	Scripture
	The Lament of Moab	Isa 15
	The Overthrow of Ephraim	Isa 28
Promise, true hope	God's Promise to the Children of His Love	Isa 35
	Song of Captivity	Ps 137
	Song of Ransom	Isa 52
	God's Love of the Church	Isa 18
	The Spread of the Gospel	Mic 4
	Thanksgiving for Mercy	Isa 7
False hopes	The Pride and Doom of Babylon	Isa 47
	The Fall of Babylon	Isa 14
	The Desolation of Babylon	Isa 13
	False Prophets	Mic 3
Redemption	Shepherd's Hymn	Ps 23
	The Desolation of the City	Lam 1
	The Fear of God the Security of Peace	Ps 128
	The Fall of the Tyrant	Isa 14
	Dwelling for the Deity	Ps 132
	Birth of Christ	Mic 5
Lie in Exile	Prayer for the Exile	Ps 126
	The Temple in Ashes	Isa 64
	Restoration from the Ruin	Isa 24
	God's Sanction Alone Gives Success	Ps 127
	Prayer of David in Exile	Ps 3
	God the Champion of His People	Ps 124
	Confidence in God's Protection	Ps 11
	The Cry of the Drowning	Ps 130
Joy in exile	Song of Solomon	Song 1:1–7
	The Season of Joy	Song 2
	The Rose of Sharon	Song 2

Simms's Sabbath Lyrics *and the Reclaiming of Sacred Time*

Topic	Title	Scripture
	Prayer in Flight	Ps 42
	Appeal from Man to God	Ps 43
	Hymn of the Departed	
	Hymn at Evening	
	Forest Worship	
From despondency to peace	Look Aloft	
	The Christian Warrior	
	Fragment from the Psalms	(Ps 19)
	The Prayer of the Parent	
	The Martyr	
	Vision of the Seraphim	Isa 6
	The Universal Power of God	Job 9
	The Triumphal March of the Sun	Ps 19
	The Quest for Peace	
	The Virgin's Grave	
	Duty	
	The World at the Sight of God	Hab 3
	Jacob Blesses Judah	Gen 49
	The Early Dead	
	Mercy's Dream	
	Plaint for the First Born	
	Despondency and Yearning	
	Children the Gift from Heaven	Ps 127
	The Shepherd's Birth	

7

Vocation and the Liberal Arts (2003)[1]

EVEN WHILE REMAINING IN the university's core curriculum in vestigial form, the liberal arts appear to the average university student, even to the graduate student, as wholly detached from any vocational meaning. They are the stuff of record keeping, of esoteric facts and texts and languages; they are the furnishings of life's attic. The liberal arts concern the university and nothing more, and the older part of the university at that. It is harmless activity for intellectuals and time-honored hoops through which the student can prove a certain intellectual agility. But, alas, it has little to do with the life one lives outside the university. This typically modern dissociation of ideas—liberal studies and vocation, ideas strongly related in logic and tradition but uncoupled by the secularizing Enlightenment—begs for repair.

Too frequently this attitude is displayed *even by the academically trained*. Recently, a candidate for dean of our theological seminary was invited to address a group of students. While holding the aim of the seminary to be practical and professional, he conceded it might be important for students to study theology, "because," he said, "you might have some smart people in your congregation." Presumably, the fewer the smart people you have in your congregation the less you need theology, it being primarily the kind of thing you do for the entertainment of people capable of engaging in that kind of talk. If your ministry, by that reasoning, is among the mentally retarded, the uneducated, or children, then theology is of little or

---

1. Originally published in *Modern Age* 45, no. 2 (2003): 123–31.

no importance! Of course, one assumes here that the value of any subject has to do with its instrumental use. The idea that it is the *learner* who needs to be changed is not even on the radar screen.

Yet the classic understanding of liberal studies centers upon the work to be done *in* the learner, not *by* the learner. The liberal arts involve the kind of study that, as Thomas Aquinas explained, is "sought for itself," and is therefore not sought for another purpose. These are thus called "free arts" (or liberal arts), in contradistinction from the arts which serve another (and presumably higher) purpose, that are properly called "mechanical or servile arts." St. Thomas expands upon this definition of the liberal arts by saying, further,

> ... the expression may specifically indicate this philosophy or wisdom which deals with the highest causes; for the final cause is also one of the highest causes.... Therefore this science must consider the highest and universal end of all things. And in this way all the other sciences are subordinated to it as an end. Hence only this science exists in the highest degree for itself.[2]

That which is truly beautiful, as Joseph Pieper reminds us, is also "attractive." The same can be said of what is "true" and what is "just" and what is noble in any other sense. What we are most concerned for in the liberal arts are not those things that we can use, but those things that can make us useful in that we are fitted for that "final" cause which has called us forth. The object is not to make us proper masters in the sense of Descartes's notion of "masters and possessors of nature," or some of Emerson's ideas of human mastery; but the object is to make us proper servants of that which is higher than we are. It orients us; but more than that, it fills us with a longing for what is rightfully an object of our longing. Liberal arts do not cause us to employ the objects of our study, but to love them, to be drawn by them, and thus to be changed ourselves. The interest of liberal arts is not in training the practical man or woman so much as in stimulating the desire for what is best.

This does not at all mean that skill is unimportant; it may in fact be central. The *trivium* of liberal studies was precisely the acquiring of skill: grammar, in order to possess the tools of investigation and representation in language; dialectic in order to empower investigation through inquiry, definition, and discrimination; and rhetoric in order to represent to the affections what is their proper object and to the will its highest good, and

2. Aquinas, *Commentary on the Metaphysics of Aristotle*, 24–25.

so that the life of the community will be ordered by what is good, true, and beautiful.

In an essay on "beauty" Josef Pieper quoted Goethe to the effect that "Beauty is not so much a fulfillment as rather a promise." Then he comments, "In other words, by absorbing beauty with the right disposition, we experience, not gratification, satisfaction, and enjoyment but the arousal of an expectation; we are oriented toward something 'not-yet-here.' He who submits properly to the encounter with beauty will be given the sight and taste not of a fulfillment but of a promise—a promise that, in our bodily existence, can never be fulfilled."[3] Yet this must not be reduced to mere "orientation" or "disposition." Rather something arouses us and accustoms our appetites and our desires to that which expands our longing. Each experience of beauty, in a poem, for instance, is only a foretaste and a sign of what is still greater. Our life is affected because it cannot help being affected; it is energized by an unearthly—rather than an earthly—hunger. Gerhart Niemeyer used to emphasize what energy was evinced in the lives of the saints: no one accomplished what was accomplished by a St. Thomas, in the realm of the intellect, or a Luther, in the realm of practical and theoretic reform, or a St. Francis, in the awakening of the spirit and a passion for life, or (I would add) a Mother Teresa in a passion for the poor and dying.

The Vocational Sentiment Embedded in Liberal Arts

This change, this "journey" of the learner, so occluded from modern eyes, constitutes the reason we need to think of liberal arts together with the idea of vocation. Though it is now neglected or diminished, it is precisely what would in the Christian tradition be called "vocation" that always gave to the education experience its dynamism. For good reason, a diminished sense of vocation leaves the province of liberal arts having to "prove its worth" in a world of pragmatic standards, one that can only understand instrumental values because it truly believes now only in power or force. This "vocation" so natural embedded in liberal education can be of immense help in restoring what was lost, in breathing life back into a passive and dead body. Niemeyer has pointed out how basic the idea of the learner being "moved" or "called" is to both religious and intellectual experience. The idea of "reason," for instance, under the regime of the Enlightenment, was critically

---

3. Pieper, *Divine Madness*, 48.

changed from its earlier form. The "creators of philosophy never spoke of reason in the way Enlightenment thinkers did." Instead,

> Parmenides experience the Is in a vision; Socrates, Plato, and other experienced being "drawn," "pulled," even "dragged" to the true reality beyond the cosmos. They respond to these experiences with something they call "the quest," "the arduous way," "the search," clearly conveying that the authority of truth is not found in themselves, nor in their method, but in their participation in a higher reality. Their attitude was one of love of the cosmos and of divine wisdom. Where in the Enlightenment do we find mention of "love" to characterize the attitude towards the cosmos or divinity? Enlightenment focuses on the objects of knowledge which mind can convert from multiplicity to unity, or from unity to composing parts, all for the sake of human control and mastery over nature.[4]

What Niemeyer described here in regard to the "creators of philosophy" corresponds in some important ways to the Christian idea of "vocation." We should dispense immediately here, of course, with what the term vocation has been reduced to in the street language of modern times. It does not refer simply to one's "occupation" or "profession" in the sense of what someone might do for a living. It is at least as broad as Martin Luther insisted upon in his essay "To the Christian Nobility of the German Nation Concerning the Reform of the Christian Estate," in which he protests the narrowing of Christian vocation to the priesthood. Even broader than the work of the Christian is the vocation or calling to the Christian life, as suggested by the Second Vatican Council's *Lumen Gentium* in recalling that "all in the Church, whether they belong to the hierarchy or are cared for by it, are called to holiness."[5] Broader still is the vision suggested by the words of *Gaudium et spes*, that faith "makes manifest the divine plan regarding man's full vocation."[6] It is in this fuller sense, the very idea that being human bears within it the insinuation of divine vocation, that I want to make the case for "vocation" as the missing element, and therefore the restorative agent for liberal arts, even as liberal arts are necessary to a humane culture.

---

4. Niemeyer, *Within and Above Ourselves*, 369.

5. "Ideo in Ecclesia omnes, sive ad Hierarchiam pertinent sive ab ea pacuntur, ad sanctitatem vocantur." *Lumen Gentium* n. 39.

6. *Gaudium et spes* n. 11.

Safeguarding a Truly Catholic Vision of the World

Vocation in the Christian Theological Tradition

Christian theology of a divine calling, or vocation, begins with the disclosure in the first chapter of Genesis that "God created man in his own image."[7] Christians, especially since Origen, one of the Greek Fathers of the Church, have understood this not as a completed act, referring it to the chronological past, nor have they seen it as a simple endowment of humanity with godlike qualities. It was understood as rooted in God's design, but also as a promise. It is dynamic rather than static; something that draws the human being toward God, rather than placing him on his own beside God.

Origen made this point by indicating the two ways in which these words are used in Genesis. First the text says, "Let us make man in our image, after our likeness."[8] Then, as God fulfills this stated intention, the text says, "So God created man in his own image, in the image of God he created him; male and female he created them."[9] Such was Origen's respect for the very words of scripture that he believed the omission of "likeness" in the second statement could scarcely have been accidental. It must have been intentional; and it must therefore have meaning.[10] Origen concluded that, while one can say that man is created in the image of God, the image is not yet perfected. That perfection of the *imago* is represented by the word *similtudo*, likeness. As Father José Alviar has stated the matter, "The task imposed by God on man upon creating him is, therefore, to become even more like the Maker, enriching and perfecting the original image." Thus the idea of "image" endows human beings with a "fundamental destiny." They experience existence in terms of a tension between what they intuit themselves to be destined for, and what they find themselves to be, between the justice and the goodness they are capable of imagining and where, in that regard, they live.

The Christian understanding of sin is often misunderstood precisely at this point. In confessing sin, we are not responding to, or face by, the "minimal requirements" of a moral life; nor are we faced with the average or typical behavior of the community. The experience of sin is rather an awareness of falling perpetually short of a destiny for which we are created,

---

7. Gen 1:27 (NRSV).
8. Gen 1:26 (RSV).
9. Gen 1:27.

10. With regard to Origen's doctrine of vocation, I have been considerably aided, and in this study am in debt to, the excellent monograph by Alviar, *Klesis*.

of something that "calls" us beyond the experience of the expectations of this life; it is an awareness of having "betrayed," in this sense, something which we have never experienced, and which yet pulls us beyond ourselves. It is tied to the experience, one might say, of vocation. As Father Alviar expressed it, in referring to the "labile existence" of the image in which the human being is made:

> It is "already" and at the same time "not yet" present. In one sense, man possesses the image from the start, as he is rational by essence; in another sense, he possesses the image tenuously, for the achievement of virtue is a contingent process. Man is expected to bring the image to fulfillment, sharing in the Word's attributes no minimally but fully.[11]

In the New Testament, and especially in the writings of St. Paul, the "vocation" is always toward a higher unifying reality, namely the body of Christ. It is furthermore an eschatological reality for which one might hope, and a reality for which one might long to suffer for its greater glory. "He must increase, but I must decrease" are words appropriate to this sentiment of a greater good calling for the suffering, longing, and diminishing of the person. The Enlightenment nation-state also calls for individual sacrifice, but it does so posing as a deliverer from the petty tyrannies of traditional authorities, such as the church, the tribe, and the family. The irony of this trade-off is apparent; for the state profits from diminishing the ties to which the individual is born, or in which the individual abides in common faith. What it accomplishes by preaching the enlargement of the individuals sphere of action and privilege is binding the individual more tightly to itself in the place of these traditional authorities. At the same time it requires the kind of sacrifice that is implied in the individual's relationship to family or community of faith.

Since the sixteenth century the state become a new kind of community. It is not a true nation, since it is made up generally of many nations, although there is a dominant national culture. Its influence then arises from the fact that it is organized in a way that dissolves what is organic and to some extent voluntary. It should not be surprising then that the concepts of "vocation" and the concept of vocation as it is embedded in the liberal arts has subsided in the public consciousness along with the rise of modern institutions. Organizations do not need such ideas or experiences, but organic communities do. It should not be surprising, therefore, that

11. Ibid., 27.

modernity has been marked by the exaggeration of the freedoms of the individual, the alienation of the person, the dissolution of families, and a culture of pathological loneliness: for these features are in the very design of the organized society which replaces the organic society.

Monastic Influence on the Idea of Vocation

There is no need here to rehearse the fact, lamented by various commentators on the doctrine of Christian vocation, that the concept has, by stages, been reduced to the calling to the monastic life, to the life of the priesthood or the religious orders. Protestants recall Luther's broadening of the idea of vocation to include the work of the laborer and the magistrate, as well as the minister of the church. The lesson was not a new one, but the emphasis was new. Calvin's genius for gaining the balance in a Christian teaching was applied to the idea of vocation as having a double focus, one upon the earthly duty and the other upon the heavenly destiny. In this way the common tasks of the Christian, as well as those more greatly honored in society, are held in new esteem. He writes in the *Institutes* of those tasks as bearing a certain nobility when the person "will bear and swallow the discomforts, vexations, weariness, and anxieties in his way of life, when he has been persuaded that the burden was laid upon him by God." In this way, "no tasks will be so sordid and base, provided you obey your calling in it, that it will not shine and be reckoned very previous in God's sight."[12]

But the broadening of the concept of vocation was seen by Dietrich Bonhoeffer to have had its own reductionistic effect. Max Weber's definition of vocation as a "limited field of [secular] accomplishment" could be seen as the failure of the Lutheran view to retain vocation as more than "the justification and sanctification of secular institutions."[13] For vocation "in the New Testament sense, is never a sanctioning of worldly institutions as such; its 'yes' to them always includes at the same time an extremely emphatic 'no,' an extremely sharp protest against the world."[14] The monastic system had at least provided the death-defying "no," even if it had failed to adequately provide the life-affirming "yes" of Christian vocation. The result of the division in Christendom, however, was seen by Bonhoeffer as having "two disastrous misunderstandings." Both misunderstandings, "the secular

---

12. *Institutes*, III, 10, 6.
13. See Bonhoeffer, *Ethics*, 250.
14. Ibid., 251.

Protestant one and the monastic one," were less than the Pauline idea of vocation deserved, and less than the church has at times seen in its fullness.

The Secular Understanding of *Imago Dei* as Endowment

Behind what is normally seen as an unwarranted reduction of the Christian idea of vocation, however, is a competing idea that is not usually fully appreciated by the biblical scholar and the theologian. The idea of the *imago dei*, with which the early formulation of *vocation* was so strongly involved, was easily taken in a sense quite different from that expressed by Origen, Augustine, Aquinas, and Luther.

The word merely needed to be spoken in order that some, who would take it to mean that the human is *endowed* with a godlike character, would find it useful in all sorts of ways. Modernity is perhaps a legacy of just such a development. For the medieval period, especially the Renaissance, is replete with examples of overweening pride in the human place in the cosmos. Giovanni Pico, Count of Mirandola (1463–1494), is one who comes readily to mind, with his influential *Oration on the Dignity of Man*. Frances Yates showed how deftly this most influential European, this leading thinker and guide of Popes and of the Medici of the Renaissance, transformed human dignity based upon the hope of overcoming fallenness into something quite different. "The fathers of the Church had placed man in a dignified position," Yates writes, "as the highest of terrestrial beings, as spectator of the universe, as the microcosm containing within himself the reflection of the macrocosm." But Pico's oration goes a step further. "All these orthodox notions are in the oration on the Dignity of Man," but these ideas are used to support the notion of the human being as "Magus, as operator, having within him the divine creative power, and the magical power of marrying heaven and earth" with the anticipation that since once human beings held such powers, they could once again become the masters of nature through the intellect, and this new Man could come into his proper role as "a divine being."[15]

---

15. Yates, *Bruno and the Hermetic Tradition*, 111.

Safeguarding a Truly Catholic Vision of the World

Max Weber's "Science as a Vocation"

That such speculation about the nature of humanity was given many subtle—and not so subtle—variations is to be expected. The strength of the idea of the human being's endowed preeminence in nature, and power over nature, is shown by the continuation of Renaissance themes into the Enlightenment idea of science as the power of becoming "the masters and possessors of nature" (Descartes). A later indication, however, of a certain Renaissance and Enlightenment theme coming with undiminished influence into our own times is the early twentieth-century impact of a certain address by Max Weber. This address, as a matter of fact, could be seen as a contemporary updating and reframing of Pico della Mirandola's oration on the Dignity of Man. Like its Renaissance prototype, it is a peculiar blend of science and theology.

In 1919, Max Weber was invited to give an address to students on "Science as a Vocation." This address comes down to us as both a very strange paper and an extraordinarily influential one. The influence of the piece speaks for itself. It has fostered a way of thinking about our world and the place of formal studies in that world that remains a strong prejudice in contemporary thinking. And I mean by "prejudice" not blind bigotry as it has come to be used, but a settled conviction that, as Edmund Burke said, is necessary to conversations of a very high order. And when I saw that it is "strange," I am not suggesting that it is merely eccentric and for that reason easily dismissed. I happen to hold the rather conventional view that Max Weber is one of the most formidable intellectuals of the past century. As Leo Strauss said, "Whatever may have been his errors, he is the greatest social scientist of our century." What I mean by strange is that it is profoundly ironic. It seems to advance the cause of modern science only be resurrecting the theology of polytheism. Weber properly sees that the questions of "meaning" raised by modern science are necessarily theological questions. But rather than attempt to answer those questions—which he admits science is incapable of doing—he said that "the different value systems of the world stand in conflict with one another."[16] The religious journey of the world that has led to monotheism, as well as mono-ethics, and which "dethroned this polytheism in favor of 'the One that is necessary,'" has been faced with new contingencies in a modern world. Weber could as easily have said that the rationalizing and disenchantment of the world that are

---

16. Lassman, Velody, and Martins, eds., *Weber's 'Science as a Vocation,'* 22.

Vocation and the Liberal Arts (2003)

by-products of monotheism have now been superannuated; but because of an extraordinary reversal of worldviews, we must abandon monotheism and along with it, mono-ethics. What he did say was that "just as Hellenic man sacrificed on this occasion to Aphrodite and on another to Apollo, and above all as everybody sacrificed to the gods of his city—things are still the same today, but disenchanted and divested of the mythical but inwardly genuine flexibility of those customs." For instance, he argues,

> What man would presume to "refuse scientifically" the morality of the Sermon on the Mount, for example the sentence, "resist no evil" or the image of turning the other cheek? And yet it is clear from the perspective of this world that here an undignified morality is being preached. The choice is between the religious dignity which this morality confers and the dignity of man, which preaches something quite different; "Resist evil, for otherwise you will share the responsibility for its supremacy." For each individual, according to his ultimate standpoint, one is the devil and the other God, and the individual must decide which *for him* is God and which the devil. And so it is in all aspects of life.[17]

It is no wonder, then, that he quotes John Stuart Mill favorably to the effect that "if one proceeds from pure experience, one arrives at polytheism."[18] It is also important to see that the idea of vocation tends toward monotheism, as does the idea of liberal arts that always refers back to first principles and to higher unifying ideals. What is described her is the abstract design of a multicultural world view, where "different value systems of the world stand in conflict with one another."[19]

It is serendipitous, from the standpoint of a research into culture and the sources of community, that in this essay a major shaper of modern thought beings together the issues of higher education, the vocation of human beings as "knowers" (scientists), and the meaning of the human community.[20] It is remarkable, further, that we have at hand an oration (that of

---

17. Ibid., 23.
18. Ibid., 22.
19. Ibid.
20. With regard to the "researcher into culture and the sources of community" I also have in mind that every Christian (and one might easily make an argument for every monotheist in this case, but I happen to be a Christian and a student of theology) is a researcher into culture and the sources of community. This is so inasmuch as all who, through the teachings and experience of faith, place themselves in the midst of a community practice (culture) and trust in the sources of community (love and justice, issuing

Pico della Mirandola) appearing at the dawn, rather than at the decadent end, of modernity, that reflects upon these same issues in rather comparable ways. In between we have an abundance of evidence that the rhetoric of the divine powers and privileges of the human being work no matter how preposterous the form in which it comes to us. And preposterous is not too strong a term to describe Emerson's *Nature* or Kant's invitation for every man to think for himself, or Locke's presumption in making a *tabula rasa* (as Eric Voegelin put it) of two thousand years of Christian intellectual history replacing it with "an analysis of the New Testament as if it were a book that had been published yesterday."[21]

Vocation, Liberal Arts, and the Possibility of Community

What is missing is not the simple idea of community, about which postmodernists never tire of speaking. Rather, the distinction that needs to come to light more clearly is the nature of that body, whether it is based on "love," and the longing for a higher unity—a basis for communing—or whether it is based on "equality" expressed as rights, which is a kind of calculation. In one, the person is indispensable. In the other, the individual is interchangeable, for if all are equal in every way, one will do as well as the other. But if we belong in different ways and for different purposes to the same body, then our gifts are needed and our lives are valued precisely because we are different.

The distinction here is highlighted when we once again detect the theological idea of *vocatio* as it is related to the liberal arts and to the task of a university. Through love, it is the lover that is changed, rather than the object of love. Thus, the learner—or the one who responds to vocation in this larger sense—is not "equipped" in the sense of being fitted for instrumental power, but is enlarged in the sense of becoming capable of refinement, discrimination, generosity of spirit, a discerning pathos, and a heightened expectation. The experience of beauty is not, as Pieper and Franz Rosensweig explain, the experience of perfection but the provoking of a suffering for what is perfect. Just so, the one who is "called" and experiences life as a "call," can be said to suffer for that which is higher, nobler, better. It is the experience of love, hope, father, the theological virtues: each

---

peace), find themselves the brother and sister of a catholic humanity and participants in (rather than masters of) nature.

21. Voegelin, *Revolution and the New Science*, 173.

Vocation and the Liberal Arts (2003)

of which expresses a certain "longing for" and a certain "suffering for" that which is unknown in the sense that we have "mastered" it, but known in the sense that it has laid hold of our affections and our intellectual anticipation. It is unknown as an instrumental thing, as something subject to our power, but known as the object of one's longing and suffering love.

What has happened, then, to liberal arts over time underlines as no other development—no matter how much more dramatic—the tension between two competing visions of community life, and that which forms community. These rivals have not just emerged in modern times; it is only that their rivalry has been clarified as never before. The options between them have always been present. The rivalry is between power in the sense of force as the means of social organization, and affection as the tie that binds people together, that binds them to their proper tasks, that binds them in creative and loving ways to their places and their things. Of course, both of these principles have their place, practically speaking, in the world as we know it. Power as coercion has its place because the world is fallen. The power of affection or love has its place because the world longs for redemption. Yet they are necessarily competing options, and each appeals to us with ecumenical designs; each is ambitious in an empire-building way, seeking to complete itself with world domination. The Christian hope is that love will win out, binding everything together in a web of divine *vocatio* –all things called to their proper place in a celebration where it is possible to:

> Let the sea roar, and all that fills it;
> The world and those who live in it.
> Let the floods clap their hands;
> Let the hills sing together for joy.[22]

And because this *vocatio*, this call, has affected the world so strongly, it has often played into the hands of the rival, for force offers immediacy, it short-circuits those features of vocation which are characterized by a suffering-longing, a resistance to distraction, and a quest that leads into an eternal mystery. Power is the siren call that offers relief from the suffering of love: but it also proves the truth of Kafka's fifty-word story entitled *The Sirens*:

> These are the seductive voices of the night; the Sirens, too, sang that way. It would be doing them an injustice to think that they wanted to seduce; they knew they had claws and sterile wombs,

---

22. Ps 98:7, 8 (NRSV).

and they lamented this aloud. They could not help it if their laments sounded so beautiful.[23]

In a fallen world power is needed as a prophylactic against violence. And though it is always sterile and unproductive of those virtues most needed in the social life, it tempts us to believe that it can accomplish quickly what love does only through patience and what it only fully accomplishes at the End of All Things. Liberal arts, on the other hand, restored to their proper relationship to the idea and experience of vocation, are a needed constant reminder of what is the true nature of ties that bind a people together and that call them along with the world itself to their God.

---

23. Kafka, *Parables and Paradoxes*, 93.

8

As Bad as We Get[1]

APOLOGISTS FOR THE "GAY community" who attempt to harmonize their sexual agenda with Christianity take comfort in the rarity of explicit prohibitions of homosexual acts and declare them unrepresentative of the biblical teaching. (But then, one would be hard-pressed to find such prohibitions of fraud, prostitution, child abuse, slave trading, sexual harassment, price fixing, lynching, racial discrimination, and any number of acts for which no one needs to find express prohibition in the Bible to be convinced that Scripture is against them.)

In this debate, one side maintains that homosexual behavior is not compatible with biblical teaching, while the other side holds that it is in harmony with—indeed approval is demanded by—the theme of love and inclusiveness in the New Testament. The latter sometimes claim to side with Jesus against Paul, since Jesus at least does not mention homosexuality while Paul does. But there they have a problem, for Paul makes the case for inclusiveness most explicitly, and Jesus spoke explicitly about what would happen to those who taught against the law. They want to embrace Paul's teachings on inclusiveness while rejecting his other teachings, and take heart from what the Gospels neglect to mention while ignoring what they do.

---

1. Originally published in *Touchstone* 17.5 (June 2004).

Safeguarding a Truly Catholic Vision of the World

The Biblical Pattern

Given these arguments, what is more needed than finding a consistent teaching in Scripture and then applying it to what has become a crucial modern moral issue—and one, furthermore, that strikes at the core of modern human self-understanding? Or are we left with the answer of the Episcopal theologian recently interviewed on MSNBC, who flatly refused to be questioned about Scripture's teaching, so "subtle and complicated," she claimed, were the issues?

The answer, I think, can be found not only in what Scripture says about homosexuality but also in the way it uses homosexuality. The biblical condemnation of homosexual acts is not a violation of its real teaching of love and inclusiveness, but in part a sign of what sin is and does, and how it so disorders and corrupts human desire that we do not want the created nature through which God will bring us true love and true inclusivity.

I will illustrate this from the Pentateuch (Genesis 18 and 19), the Deuteronomic history (Judges 17ff), and the Pauline epistles (Romans 1). In the Old Testament especially, but also in the New, homosexuality is treated like most moral issues, within the story of humanity, a nation, and a regenerate community, all of which have an essentially moral vocation: a vocation to be holy, righteous, and reconciled with God, nature, and each other.

The problem depicted in each of the three passages is not only that men are so depraved that they have left behind the natural desire for women, but also that the social situation is now irredeemable without drastic intervention and judgment. Homosexuality is a sign that the social situation has gotten that bad. To this end, the writers typically use it as a means of illustrating the anti-naturalism of sin: the vaporous sexual imagination that rejects the natural relation to the other (the other sex) and instead seeks union with the same (as a nearer reflection of the self).

The result is even at first glance obvious: an unfruitful relation that begets nothing and denies the power of sex in relation to one truly other than the self, and thus destroys the community itself. Scripture never sees created nature as antagonistic to God's purposes, but as the context in which those purposes—including human happiness—are to be pursued. Scripture opposes the actions that deny nature, and thus deny true human happiness: when the human imagination refuses to accept the limits (and the benefits) of nature, but seeks to overcome nature to satisfy its fallen fantasies.

We can see this in each of the passages I have listed. Each: (1) uses homosexuality to illustrate the degree to which a community, or mankind itself, has declined in evil and disorder; (2) describes homosexuality as not only the object of judgment but also the very form of the judgment; (3) sees it as a rejection of nature; and (4) understands it as a violation against community.

The destruction of Sodom and Gomorrah (Genesis 18 and 19) draws the reader into a consideration of the possibility that human evil might become so intractable that it overreaches even the mercy of God. The story is not about homosexuality by itself, but about the fact of human evil and its perilous end, as shown in the picture of a disorder deeply woven into the community's life. Abraham's bargaining with the divine messengers makes clear that if there are fifty, or forty-five, or forty, or thirty, or twenty, or ten who are righteous, the Lord will not destroy the city—the length of the passage serving to underline the willingness of God to bring judgment only in the most extreme case of the community's depravity.

The two angels who proceed to Sodom are offered hospitality by Lot. "But before they lay down, the men of the city, the men of Sodom, both the young and the old, all the people to the last man, surrounded the house; and they called to Lot, 'Where are the men who came to you tonight? Bring them out to us, that we may know them.'" Lot, highlighting the indelible character of their perversity, says to them: "I beg you, my brethren, do not act so wickedly. Behold I have two daughters who have not known man; let me bring them out to you, and do to them as you please; only do nothing to these men, for they have come under the shelter of my roof."

The ancient Near-Eastern obligation of a host to his guest, of course, plays a part in this. And though we are naturally shocked by the offer of Lot's virgin daughters to the crowd of men, this device is a common one when the biblical writer is giving an account of the depth of wickedness to which a community might descend. The point is that these men are so depraved that they do not want the women.

No King in Israel

We find a similar episode in the Deuteronomic account (Judges 17ff.), which depicts Israel's downwardly spiraling society. The story is punctuated with the words: "In those days there was no king in Israel; every man did what was right in his own eyes." It tells of a deeply disordered society, one that had reached such depths that the people of Israel are represented as asking "Tell us, how was this wickedness [which included the brutal murder of a concubine by a sexually wanton crowd of men] brought to pass?"

At the climax of the story, a Levite arrives with his concubine and his male servant at a place near Jerusalem, which was at this time still occupied by the Jebusites. They decline to lodge with the Jebusites, who were foreigners, but travel farther so as to stay with their own countrymen in Gibeah. This point is significant, because the story goes on to show that the Israelites had become worse than the foreign Jebusites. An old man takes in the trio. Then, "As they were making their hearts merry, behold, the men of the city, base fellows, beset the house round about, beating on the door; and they said to the old man, the master of the house, 'Bring out the man who came into your house, that we may know him.'"

This passage mirrors the story of Sodom, suggesting a literary convention that depicts the depth of evil in a society by the stubborn presence of homosexual desire. Its stubbornness is underlined in a slightly different fashion in the balance of this passage, but it is clearly devised so that it stresses the pathology of corporate sin that is so entrenched that it becomes inescapable. These lines follow:

> And the man, the master of the house, went out to them and said to them, "No, my brethren, do not act so wickedly; seeing that this man has come into my house, do not do this vile thing. Behold, here are my virgin daughter and his concubine; let me bring them out now. Ravish them and do with them what seems good to you; but against this man do not do so vile a thing."

In this story, the city is not destroyed as is the case for Sodom, but the concubine is thrown out of the house, abused and murdered by the crowd of men. So once again, deep disorder, the rebellion of sin, is disclosed by the presence of homosexual practice, and comes to fruition in violence. In both passages there is no extensive discussion of the depravity of a society. In each case, one is informed of the depth of depravity by reference to the presence of homosexual aggressiveness.

Paul does little more than draw upon this Old Testament imagery when he unfolds the nature of sin in Romans 1. He is using homosexual practice, which in his mind is self-evidently corrupt, in order to explain and condemn the sin that corrupts all of humanity. As in the passages from Genesis and Judges, homosexuality serves to illustrate the human predicament and the deadliness of the unredeemed human imagination. It is the stock biblical illustration of social corruption en extremis.

Thus, he explains that sin is rooted in self-deception, and becomes its own judgment as "God gives them up" to their self-destructive practices. That sin and judgment are one and the same is proven, according to Paul, by the extremes to which the human imagination leads to "dishonorable passions": "Their women exchanged natural relations for unnatural, and the men likewise gave up natural relations with women and were consumed with passion for one another, men committing shameless acts with men and receiving in their own persons the due penalty for their error."

Thus, not only is sin forgetful of the fact that it is God who is the author of nature, but the logic of sin is that it first draws a person to worship nature, and then to turn against it in violence and vanity.

The Misuse of Judgment

Reflecting our modern flight from moral judgment, the exegete is likely to fall into one of two errors in assessing the place of homosexuality in Scripture: to avoid judgment or to apply it only to others. A common error for modern society is the assumption that making moral distinctions between right and wrong is itself reprehensible. It is true that it is dangerous, and gives rise to the opposite exegetical error: the view that when Paul speaks of homosexual practice, he is speaking of someone else.

Yet New Testament teachings against judgment are not a warning against judgment as such, but against judgment that does not begin with the self. "First take the log out of your own eye," Jesus teaches, "and then you will see clearly to take the speck out of your brother's eye." Paul is not trying to show that homosexuality, acted out, is an especially heinous sin, but that all sin is like homosexuality. Thus, we are called not to examine the sins of others so much as to examine our own.

That being the case, it is well to remind ourselves that while all of us sin, each of us is more inclined to sin in one way rather than another. One person is more tempted by greed and theft, another by lust and adultery, and yet another by anger and murder. It should be no surprise, nor should it make any difference, if it is ever proven that genetics burdens some of us with an inclination toward homosexuality, since we are all similarly burdened (whatever the source) with our individual inclinations to lust, anger, greed, envy, sloth, and the whole list—any one of which is capable of bringing us to Hell.

Safeguarding a Truly Catholic Vision of the World

For that reason alone, the Christian response to those burdened with the temptation of homosexuality is always one of compassion for the sinner and repentance for our own sins: compassion because we are equally burdened (if in a different way), and repentance because the rise of homosexuality among us is a sign that sin has corrupted the whole of society and each of us with it.

9

Can Postmodernism Be Used as a Template for Christian Theology? (2004)[1]

THE CLAIM THAT GENERATIONS transition progressively from one distinctive era to the next, the periodization of history, is a peculiarly modern device. Special problems attend this habit when it is claimed that modernity itself has been, or is in the process of being, eclipsed by yet another distinct and inexorable period of history. How can one tell if what is claimed as "postmodern" is in fact something different—especially when it seems to be marked by the same habit of periodization, the same value for novelty, and the same implied historical optimism? The problem that this presents for theology has not, I think, been sufficiently appreciated, even by those who wish, lately, to frame theology in a postmodern context.

Perhaps the problem can best be presented by raising an awareness of a certain inevitable contrast between two very different modes of approaching theology. These two modes are, first, "vocational" in form and content, or, second, one that is shaped by the primacy of "choice" in all human endeavors, even theology. Let me amplify the differences between these two, keeping in mind that the former is what I take to be most important in traditional theism, and the latter partakes of the formative influence of the Enlightenment.

Until early in the modern period, advances in philosophy and theology borrowed heavily from the sentiment of vocation. Ideas were not true because they captured the imagination, but they captured the imagination

[1]. Originally published in *Christian Scholar's Review* 33, no. 3 (2004): 293–309.

because they were true. The pre-modern idea of discovering what is true seems, from the witness of those who articulated their discovery, a necessary thing: for the reality itself calls forth an inward assent. The attitude of the thinker is described as "hungering and thirsting" rather than as inventive, resourceful, imaginative. The thinker is receptive. He is in no wise merely creative or imaginative. Of the mysteries of time, St. Augustine would say, "My soul is on fire to know this most intricate enigma."[2] Augustine's fire is kindled, however, by the mystery outside of him, not by the natural disposition of his passions. Of truth found in Scripture, Clement of Alexandria would say, "Scripture helps to kindle a fire in, our soul, it directs our natural sight . . . it rouses to new life our natural endowment."[3] Hilary of Poitiers spoke of what drove the thinker on as "a natural yearning . . . encouraged by some hope of an everlasting happiness."[4] Applying this matter to the saving disposition of faith, Luther said in his Heidelberg Disputation of 1518 that free will could not "remain in a state of innocence, much less do good, in an active capacity, but only in its passive capacity."[5] In fact, Luther thought of his whole reformation movement as nothing more than a passive listening to the Word of God, hardly as "an imaginative new project in theology," such as we frequently hear of contemporary movements. He said, "I simply taught, preached, wrote God's Word; otherwise I did nothing. And then while I slept, or drunk Wittenburg beer . . . the Word so greatly weakened the papacy that never a prince or emperor did such damage to it. I did nothing. The Word did it all."[6] All of these illustrate what I would call a "vocational" disposition toward truth, for we are "called forth" into a reality that exists beyond our present dwelling. One should not misunderstand this as the comprehension of truth, but simply as a movement toward what is true.

Modern thinkers, on the other hand, are frequently described as imaginative, resourceful, inventive, and in a word, fully responsible for the product of their thinking. From Francis Bacon forward, the tendency was to understand knowledge not as a doorway into reality by which one might enter into and participate in that reality, but knowledge was understood as a "power" by which one becomes (in the language of Descartes) the "master

---

2. Augustine, *Confessions*, XI, 28.
3. Clement of Alexandria, *Stromateis*, I, 10 (4), 29.
4. Hilary of Poitiers, *Trinity*, 10.
5. Thesis 15, cited in Forde, *On Being a Theologian of the Cross*, 56.
6. Cited in George, *Theology of the Reformers*, 53.

Can Postmodernism Be Used as a Template for Christian Theology? (2004)

and possessor of nature."[7] Immanuel Kant would speak of "Enlightenment" as leaving the immaturity whereby one depends upon the tutelage of others and having "the courage to use your own intelligence."[8] He would speak of man as generating "entirely out of himself everything going beyond the mechanical organization of his animal existence," that "he partake of no other happiness or perfection than that which he provides for himself, free of instinct, by means of his own reason."[9] Herbert Marcuse would speak of the growth of this notion of control by the autonomous human being:

> Protestantism and the bourgeois revolutions proclaimed the freedom of thought and conscience. They were the sanctioned forms of contradiction [to the social order]—oftcn the only ones—and the most precious refuge of hope. Only rarely and in exceptional cases did bourgeois society dare to infringe on this refuge. Soul and mind were (at least officially) considered holy and awesome. Spiritually and mentally, man was supposed to be as autonomous as possible.[10]

Of course, this notion of "control" gave rise to Tower-of-Babel-like fantasies that dominated the twentieth century. Perhaps no one spoke in this mode more succinctly than the architect Walter Gropius in the early years of that unfortunate century: "Together let us desire, conceive, and create the new structure of the future, which will embrace architecture and sculpture and painting in one unity and which will one day rise toward heaven from the hands of a million workers like the crystal symbol of a new faith."[11]

This change of orientation experienced in modern times is a profound one: moving the human being from the role of receptive discoverer, listener, and responder to the world, to that of shaper, fashioner, even creator of the world—the *maître et possesseur* of nature. This change, so profound

---

7. The dictum "knowledge is power" is often attributed to Francis Bacon and is the theme of much of his writing; the idea that science "makes us the masters and possessors of nature" is from Descartes, *Discours de la Méthode*, 634.

8. Immanuel Kant, "What Is Enlightenment?" (1784) in *The Philosophy of Kant*, 145.

9. Immanuel Kant, *Idee zu einter allgemeinen Geschichte in weltbürgerlicher Absicht*. Cited in Marcuse, *Negations*, 102.

10. Marcuse, *Negations*, xii.

11. Gropius, "Programme of the staatliches Bauhaus in Weimar" (1919), in *Programmes and Manigestoes on Twentieth-Century Architecture*, 25. Cited in Grenz, *Primer on Postmodernism*, 23.

and yet so firmly embedded in the language of post-Enlightenment people, gives us a criterion by which to adjudge something truly modern. For the truly modern is that which no longer possesses the imaginative resources with which to understand how the human being participates in the created order. Instead, modern imagination has conjured the notion of human existence lodged, somehow, above and outside of nature and history. In this world, of course, the language of vocation loses its potency precisely to the extent that there is no voice, really, to call men and women into participation. They are not properly called; instead, they choose and thus order their own lives.

Thus, up until modern times, the language of philosophy and theology evoke this essentially religious experience of vocation. But in modern times, though the option is present in every time and place, there has been a widespread rejection of this experience and the systematic effort to replace it with an "elective" view of things. In one, men and women respond to a "calling," thus discovering a reality that was greater than they knew. In the other, men and women understand themselves to be "constructing" something, to be "creating" a new world or a changed world, or perhaps even a Utopian world. An element of the question before us is whether "postmodern"—in any of its currently fashionable definitions—is anything other than modern. Now, many people think of the highly publicized "postmodern" movement—in the arts, in popular belief, in codes of conduct, in architecture, in philosophy, and in theology—as a legitimate successor, perhaps the only possible successor, to modern life. Interestingly enough, I think it is in the juxtaposition of postmodernism with a vigorous sense of the "vocational" ordering of life that we see these assumptions put to a genuine test. My sense is that they are irreconcilable. Others, however, would like to see theology recast in what has come to be called (falsely, I think) a postmodern "context." That project is what I wish to examine next in order to test if the sentiment of "vocation" is not more truly a path that delivers us from the decay of modern life, without at the same time rejecting it for sentimental and reactionary purposes.

In theology, a number of very different movements attach themselves in some way to "postmodernism." On the left, theologically, is the postliberal theology exemplified by George Lindbeck's attempt to base theology on Wittgenstein's linguistic and cultural insights. Or there is the liberation theology of Gustavo Gutierrez, Juan Luis Segundo, and others. Again, one might look at the "revisionist" theology of David Tracy, or to some style of feminist theology, or even go back to the radical "God is dead" theology of the sixties. But to bring the instance of "postmodernism" into closest proximity with a view that describes itself as "evangelical" might be most productive in finding whether the "vocational" view of life and the "elective" view of life are still, in what is styled "postmodernism," in contention with one another. To test the harmony, or indeed the disharmony, of these ideas—postmodernism and "vocation"—I wish to look briefly at the work of three who have attempted to bring together evangelicalism (which is strongly marked in its heritage by a vocational view of life) and postmodernism (with its dependence, as we shall see, upon a radically elective view of life). These three are Stanley Grenz, John Franke, and the late James McClendon.[12]

Postmodernism in an Evangelical "Context"

Professors Stanley Grenz and John R. Franke are the authors of *Beyond Foundationalism: Shaping Theology in a Postmodern Context*. This book is certainly one of the more helpful ones in proposing clearly how evangelical theology might take postmodern developments seriously and constructively in an attempt to articulate theology for the contemporary world. The attempt itself is interesting for a number of reasons. First, evangelicalism, in its American expression, like its cousin "fundamentalism," is essentially a critique of modernity, which postmodernism of almost any style also claims to be. Yet, second, evangelicals of almost any style make strange bedfellows with the likes of the most famous postmodernists—such as Derrida and Foucault—who deride anything so highly charged with "universal significance" as the Bible, which evangelicals typically claim to be foundational. Third, either evangelicals who hope to "shape theology in a postmodern context" have subscribed to the dictum that "the enemy of my enemy is my friend" or they have assumed, as people have been persuaded to assume since the dawn of modernity, that society rolls from one era to the next like a locomotive and boxcars on a track and that theology only has the option of going backward or forward, just like that locomotive. And if it wishes to "relate" to the world in which it lives, it must keep up with that train, there being no other options at all—only backward (which is seen as "negative") or forward (which is progressive and therefore good). Of course, this last

---

12. To date, the best critical assessment of evangelical postmodernism is found in Erickson, *Postmodernising the Faith*.

thought sounds so strongly related to the very modern (not especially postmodern) idea of historical progress, that one suspects that what is called postmodernity—by its very name *post*modern—has not fully escaped the spell of modernity.

Grenz and Franke claim, as one might expect evangelicals to claim, that postmodemity need not be linked necessarily with its most radical European spokesmen, that one in fact might include any number of figures who are simply critics of modernity and its excesses such as "its quest for certain, objective, and universal knowledge, along with its dualism and its assumption of the inherent goodness of knowledge."[13] They include other critics of modernity such as Nancey Murphy, Alvin Plantinga, Nicolas Wolterstorff, Alasdair MacIntyre, and Stephen Toulmin, as well as a number of others. Of course, if the lowest common denominator of "postmodernity" included only the requisite criticism of modernity, then they might have included others who are perhaps even stronger critics of modernity than some of those they named: as, for instance, Eric Voegelin in political philosophy, Thomas Oden and Jürgen Moltmann in theology, Flannery O'Connor, Walker Percy, Evelyn Waugh, T. S. Eliot, and the whole gang of "Fugitives" in literature, and then added Richard Weaver and George Panichas in cultural and literary criticism. Yet, their list of "postmodernists" is more selective than just the "critics of modernity." It is inclusive instead of a "certain" critique of modernity, one which I think we would do well to investigate whether in fact it has anything to do with the vocation of the church. And it is that style of postmodernity that we have to subject to our scrutiny before we can agree or disagree that such a style is suitable for Christian thinking.

First of all, we have at the very least to suspend judgment on the notion, so easily taken as self-evident by postmodern writers, that time has so inevitably and inexorably moved into this new mode that we are imprisoned in our era, as on a boxcar running along some chronological railway, and are not free to engage the world and its changes in any other way. If we cannot suspend this notion, at least long enough to have a discussion about what is now called postmodernity and what it has to do with Christian theology, then I will persist in suspecting that we are not talking about *post*-modernity at all, but about modernity, with all its faith in historical optimism, even though it is shorn of some (but not all) of its most recognizable characteristics. I will suspect that what is called postmodernity here is

---

13. Grenz and Franke, *Beyond Foundationalism*, 22.

just modernism on life-support. It looks like a rejection of every feature of modernity that might appear to any thinking person as a threadbare and bankrupt cliché—such as individualism and instrumental reason. At the same time, however, it is but the desperate attempt to cling to the very essence of modernity, which is its offer of human autonomy, of *choice*.

"Chastened Rationality" and the Task of Theology

Nevertheless, Grenz and Franke tell us that postmodernism is "best understood as referring to the rejection of the central features of modernity."[14] Let us examine their case. Under the heading of "chastened rationality and the demise of foundationalism," they see postmodern thought as marked by "the transition from a realist to a constructivist view of truth and the world," by the "loss of metanarrative," or the capacity to include all stories into one world-encompassing story, and especially by the "rejection of epistemological foundaitonalism," which might mean either a foundationalism based on subjective experience (as one finds in liberal theology) or one based on an error-free Bible (among fundamentalists). And it means the rejection of the search for certainty that, ever since John Dewey, has been projected back upon the Enlightenment (seventeenth and eighteenth centuries).

Dewey's argument for the "quest for certainty" put forward in his Gifford lectures of 1929 had become a cliché in the twentieth century, and many thinkers (and in this case Grenz and Franke) do not question it, but move from there to the rejection of "foundations," which Dewey suggested was attributable to the psychological desire for stability in the tumultuous early modern period.[15] That the quest for "first principles" is so ancient and ubiquitous that it might be attributable simply to the necessities of ordered thought is not denied, but neither is it explored. It does not occur, among those who take Dewey and his successors at their word, that the search for "first principles" does not commit the thinker to the notion of an unalterable and perfectly knowable beginning point; instead, it is more often agreed, along with St. Thomas Aquinas, that what is first in the order of being is last in the order of knowing. Nor is the thought entertained that there was an enormous difference between the modern desire to find

---

14. Ibid., 21.

15. Dewey, *Quest for Certainty*. See especially the first two chapters: "Escape from Peril" and "Philosophy's Search for the Immutable."

foundations that are intramundane and subjective and the earlier idea of reason grounded in the common experience of nature and the soul, or the uncommon gift of divine revelation. In other words, the perception that cognitive "foundations" is a feature of modernity is never questioned, and the assertion that modernity has, on this account, gotten itself into a bind and must find other ways of "constructing" reality seems the most logical conclusion. The problem, as I see it, is that the various trends of thought are neatly labeled and accepted and even the Christian postmodernists innocently go on from there.

Once the adopted reading of history is in place, it is enough simply to evoke the name "foundationalists" to lump together all sorts of philosophical and non-philosophical methods, from Descartes to Schleiermacher to American fundamentalists, and dismiss them as seekers for a "Holy Grail."[16] What literally all of these quite different, and in fact otherwise irreconcilable, thinkers do is now discredited, which of course saves us the trouble of having to think about the arguments of *each* of these thinkers. Time, and with it the *certainty* of progress, has moved on to the next phase, leaving behind the now dated discussions of a whole gaggle of liberal and evangelical modernists, Cartesians and Hobbists, conservatives, fundamentalists, and dispensationalists, leaving us with a "quest for an alternative epistemology."[17] By the time we get to this point, the field has been swept clean of any serious contenders and the way is open to all kinds of "creative" possibilities.

At this juncture, Grenz and Franke, like a number of others, introduce alternative "non-foundational" epistemologies. First there is the familiar coherentist formula that, rather than "picturing human knowledge as a building" that rests upon a certain foundation, thinks instead of the body of knowledge as "a network, in which beliefs come together to form an integrated belief system."[18] The idea that knowledge is a "web of belief" or a "nest of beliefs" or, more abstractly, a "conceptual scheme,"[19] is to suggest that what occurs in the knower, namely an effort to bring knowledge together into a coherent whole—a natural enough effort, and one that no one can avoid to some degree—is the full extent of what can be known. These

---

16. Grenz and Franke, *Beyond Foundationalism*, 38.
17. Ibid., 38ff.
18. Ibid., 39.
19. These metaphors are ascribed mainly to the works (in turn) of W. V. Quine, Wesley A. Kort, and of a critic of the system, Donald Davidson. See ibid., 39.

coherentists were "joined in their critique of foundationalism" by Charles Pierce, William James, and (one that these authors do not mention) John Dewey—the Pragmatists. For these, following close upon the assumption of generations of Empiricists, there are no "final causes" or "ends" toward which knowledge is oriented. Rather, one is guided by the "end in view" (Dewey), the subject of final ends being as elusive as foundations and meaning practically the same thing.

Grenz and Franke realize, of course, that such formulations as these hardly leave room for anything resembling theology. Coherent and pragmatic views of the world are not necessarily theistic and are in some ways made more convincing without the messiness of a Creator and a Redeemer, whose very presence tends to upset coherence and to interject values that are other than pragmatic. At this point, they turn to the theologian Wolfhart Pannenberg, whom they say has applied "noncorrespondence epistemological theories" in the study of God. Yet, for Pannenberg, the coherence of knowledge lies in the reality of God, whose disclosure depends upon an eschatological vantage point. All of this, however, brings us back to a very pre-Enlightenment (not so much post-modern) understanding of the human progress toward truth which is only fully disclosed in God, who is not fully known until the end when God becomes all and in all. So Pannenberg has not clearly freed himself of aspects of foundationalism. He is a realist. He "shares the older theological goal of discovering universal truth." The problem is that "such an enterprise . . . is impossible to accomplish," and Pannenbcrg is therefore caught in the tension of a "theological method that is nonfoundational yet committed to a realist metaphysic."[20]

At this point, the authors turn to George Lindbeck, who reintroduces Wittgenstein into a theology that escapes the older agenda of discovering universal truth, but is constituted by the "cultural-linguistic" formation of community. In this "coherentism [with] a Wittgensteinian twist,"[21] the task of theology is changed from that of discovering a truth on which to found community to that of constituting a truth within which a community can dwell. This insight becomes critical for the program outlined in the Grenz and Franke book (subtitled "Shaping Theology in a Postmodern Context"), a book almost ending with the words that "theologians assist the church in the world-construction business we share."[22]

20. Ibid., 45.
21. Ibid.
22. Ibid., 273.

Safeguarding a Truly Catholic Vision of the World

Reading between the lines, and since I also know personally one of the authors who strikes me as a genuine Christian with perfectly orthodox intentions, I can see that the sentiment of "realism" (that there is in fact a reality that underlies and judges our efforts at knowing) and the universal truth of a God fully disclosed eschatologically is still there. They, after all, refer to their approach as "eschatological realism."[23] They even do not fully escape the language of foundationalism when they say, for instance, that the "specific task of theology . . . is to draw from the unique grammar of the biblical narrative to build a linguistic world for human habitation in the present, a world whose *basis* lies in the new creation that God is already bringing to pass."[24] The emphasis here is my own; it illustrates how the language of any approach to knowing or doing can hardly escape the use of foundational concepts, calling into question the whole notion that the proper distinction between modern and so-called postmodern thought has to do with an older and outdated scheme for discovering foundations.

The attempt to escape the very notion of foundations, however, is unsettling. And herein, I think, lies the peril of what lately goes by the name of postmodern; it is an attempt to construe the enterprise of theology so that we consider that we are "constructing" a world rather than discovering a world. There is a sense, of course, in which knowledge is the "creation" of something. It was recognized by St. Thomas Aquinas that the reason we can know anything of God at all is because God creates all that exists and that we "make" things out of what is already created, giving us a means by which we can know analogously God's relation to the created world. But this knowledge must take into consideration a certain order of knowing. As Joseph Pieper explains, the dynamic of knowing takes place between God's knowing, which he calls the "absolutely creative knowledge of God," and human knowing, which he refers to as "the non-creative, reality-conformed knowledge of man." The former knowledge is given, but the latter is received. Using the concept of "measure" to explain the difference, Pieper says,

> The creative knowledge of God gives measure but receives none (*mensurans non mensuratum*).
>
> Natural reality is at once measured and itself measuring (*mensuratum et mensurans*). But human knowledge is measured and does not give measure (*mensuratum non mensurans*); at least it

23. For instance, on 271ff.
24. Ibid., 273.

Can Postmodernism Be Used as a Template for Christian Theology? (2004)

is not what gives measure with respect to natural things, though it does so with regard to *res artificiales*, artificial things.[25]

This necessary order of knowing, one that does not construe human knowledge as "constructing" a world when in fact it can only begin feebly to "respond" to a real world, is what appears to be missing from attempts at a "postmodern" theology. It misses that succinct wisdom found in St. Augustine's pithy formula that things exist because God sees them, whereas we see them because they exist.[26] It is for this reason, I believe, that we must examine whether in fact postmodernity has been liberated from the central concerns of the Enlightenment, that of declaring, on some level at least, an emancipation from a theocentric view of the world. The legitimacy of the postmodern claim to be *post*(modern) rather than a last-ditch effort to save the essence of modernity from total discrediting is what I wish to take up next as we find evidence of it in certain theologies of the church.

Is Postmodernity Distinguishable from Modernity?

The idea of postmodernity is useful in Christian theology only under conditions of a rigorous analysis of the meaning and character of modernity. The analysis of modernity upon which several evangelical writers have based their definition of postmodernity, or upon which some have come to be thought postmodern, has been flawed in a number of important respects.

I begin with the late James McClendon, Jr., who was a noted baptist theologian (he preferred the lower case designation, which is inclusive of more than those denominations formally labeled Baptist). In his *Ethics*, which is the first volume of his three-volume *Systematic Theology*, he explores the first steps of theology. It is interesting and instructive that he does this in connection with ethics. He points out that, in the writing of theologies, especially systematic ones, ethics is usually left until last and then left out! Instead, theology is presented in terms of its theoretical foundations first, and then various topics are considered in some logical order. He began, however, with ethics. It is the practice of a believing community that must be considered first. This, of course, accords well with the modem inclination to place will before intellect—or, to say it

---

25. Pieper, *Silence of St. Thomas*, 54.
26. Alluded to also in Pieper, *Silence of St. Thomas*, 61 (*Confessions* XIII, 38 and *De Trinitate* VI, 10).

otherwise, the inclination to assume that what we "see" is derived from what we have done or made.

This is not to deny that Christian reflection may *in fact* come some time after Christian practice. But the point is that once it is time to reflect, to *theorize*, the business of the serious Christian, it seems to me, is to ask whether the practice reflects reality, not if reality reflects practice. But in this case, McClendon saw theology as founded not in the experience of the believer, or in revelation itself, or in any other reality that "comes to" the believer, but in the conviction itself. This conviction is defined as "A persistent belief such that if X (a person or community) has a conviction, it will not be easily relinquished, and it cannot be relinquished without making X a significantly different person (or community) than before."[27] Thus, a definition of theology is rendered in this way: "The discovery, understanding, and transformation of the convictions of a convictional community, including the discovery and critical revision of their relation to one another *and to whatever else there is.*"

This definition, at first sight, appears to be quite in line with the theoretical method of any other theology—the discovery, understanding, and critical revision of "whatever." But close reading shows that everything is linked to, and founded upon, *conviction itself.* It is the "discovery . . . of the convictions of a convictional community."[28] The idea that God gives measure to nature and nature gives measure to the human seeking to know is foreign to this way of thinking, for the first order of business is not receiving measure, in the sense of "seeing," but in giving measure in the sense of making. For Aquinas, the human person gives measure to the "artifice"; but for this kind of postmodern theology, all of existence is an artifice. The focus on a "theological center," McClendon has said, leads to the "rich resource for theology in the *narrative common life.*" And the appropriate "point of departure for reflection upon this narrative and common life" is "theological ethics."[29] Thus, reflection does not lead to understanding what is by virtue of having been created by God, but only what exists by virtue of having been made by human hands or the human imagination, and this in turn exists in relation to *practices*, a product of the will.

---

27. McClendon, *Ethics*, 23. The definition is lifted from the 1975 book he wrote with Smith, *Understanding Religious Convictions*, 7, 91–94.

28. McClendon, *Ethics*, 23.

29. Ibid., 27.

Can Postmodernism Be Used as a Template for Christian Theology? (2004)

If this in fact is the way of theology, then Feuerbach and Nietzsche could not have been altogether wrong. I say this, however, knowing also that McClendon has done us all good service by showing how central the practices of the Christian are to the life of the world. My disagreement comes only as it relates to the method of theology. But, as we look at the effects of so-called postmodernism, this is indeed a decisive point.

Now, I would like to return to Stanley Grenz, one of the authors of the book we briefly examined earlier. I might take Grenz's approach as a fair example of a certain openness toward postmodernity along with a certain reservation. In the last chapter of his *Primer on Postmodernism*, for instance, he argues that evangelicals stand on common ground with postmodernity in the rejection of "Enlightenment epistemology." Modernity, he says, "is built on the assumption that knowledge is certain, objective, and good."[30] The postmodern ethos calls for a new approach in the way the gospel is presented; it "requires that we embody the gospel in a manner that is *post-individualistic*, *post-rationalistic*, *post-dualistic*, and *post-noeticentric*." I want to concentrate on the first two of these "requirements" since I believe they embody the heart of the case that is made in favor of an evangelical postmodern critique of modernity. At the same time, I want to suggest why I think Grenz and others who have treated postmodernism in this way have resisted the temptation to follow it more thoroughly. The heart of my argument is this: it is a mistake to think that postmodernism, as we have come to know it in the writings of Foucault and Derrida, for instance, is in fact a critique of modernity. It is instead an attempt to save the sinking ship of modernity by throwing overboard some of its most inessential features while preserving its essence. Individualism and rationality are not, strictly speaking, features of modernity, but rather they are features of a Christian view of life that, through the filter of the Enlightenment, were made to conform to what is the heart of modernity, and of postmodernism as well. The heart of modernity is not individualism per se, but the individual without God—the autonomous individual. And it is not rationalism per se, but a rationalism that is capable of making human beings autonomous. Postmodernity as we have come to know it is perfectly loyal to the project of modernity, while posing as its critic in order to escape what would result in an authentic postmodernity—the return to the idea of a God who creates, sustains, and intercedes in life and Who is therefore the true center and anchor of our existence.

30. Grenz, *Primer on Postmodernism*, 165.

Safeguarding a Truly Catholic Vision of the World

While modernity may very well manifest a certain exaggerated form of individualism and a distinct style of rationalism, these are not in themselves features of modernity. That is to say not only that their roots go far back into the medieval period, and even into antiquity, but it is to say that once we focus on these peculiar features, we have still not gotten to the core of what makes modernity modern. The way forward, therefore, is to recognize the "red herrings" of the postmodern critique for what they are and then to expose postmodernism as merely another incarnation of the modern thesis, more antagonistic than ever to the Christian (and therefore to the human) vocation. I will summarize this case in three final steps.

1. Autonomous Individualism

Individualism, for example, is said by its postmodern critics to be one of the features of modernity under attack. Yet individualism might be taken as manifesting a very long movement—from classical and biblical times until the present—which is constituted of a gradual recognition of the dignity of the human person. Francis Fukuyama, in his essay on the triumph of liberal democracies, shows how the urge for "recognition" asserts itself over a long period of time until it is crowned by the Christian sentiment that "God *recognizes* all human beings universally, recognizes their individual human worth and dignity."[31] Long before modern times, the worth of the human person is understood to stand out from his or her "place" within the community—to such an extent that the institution of slavery, so universally practiced in antiquity, was mostly abandoned in Christian lands. The reversal of this anti-slavery sentiment came *along with* modernity. That is, the institution was revived with developments in modern times, including—and perhaps especially—the discovery and development of new lands across the Atlantic for which slave trade and slave-holding became the answer to pressing modern exigencies. Modern times marked not the exaggeration of individualism, or the exaggeration of the dignity of the human person, but in fact the partial loss of that concept. And as long as merchants were becoming wealthy, first in Spain, then prominently in England and New England, the practice of slave trade remained an important feature of the modern economy. The impetus for a reaffirmation of the human person, apart from his or her commercial value to the community, came not from modernity but from pre-modern sources.

---

31. Fukuyama, *End of History and the Last Man*, 97.

Can Postmodernism Be Used as a Template for Christian Theology? (2004)

The peculiar style of modern individualism comes not from the elevation of the dignity of the individual as much as it does from the denigration of the community. The Enlightenment was in part a product of the rise of the nation-states in Europe. The rival of this new creature, this Leviathan, this organized rather than organic social entity, was any social grouping that interposed an authority of some kind between the state and the individual. Notable among these authorities, of course, was the Church. But there was also the authority of the clan, the collegium, the regional identity of people going back to ancient times. The state therefore became the champion of the individual against any authority that oppressed individual freedoms. The seventeenth-century rhetoric against the church in any form became all the more vicious as the interests of the state and the interests of state-sponsored commerce became more prominent. The individual was eventually left free to pursue his or her own course without the petty oppressions of church and family, but the individual was also left to face the world alone.

Who can imagine, for instance, *anyone* before the Enlightenment period with its insistence that "everyone should think for himself" saying what Emerson did in *Self-Reliance*:

> Society everywhere is in conspiracy against the manhood of every one of its members. Society is a joint-stock company, in which members agree, for the better securing of his bread to each shareholder, to surrender the liberty and culture of the eater . . . . Self reliance is its aversion . . . . He who would gather immortal palms must not be hindered by the name of goodness, but must explore if it be goodness. Nothing is at lust sacred but the integrity of your own mind.[32]

There are still places in the world where this sort of sentiment would be laughed off the stage, but nonetheless it marks an unfailing characteristic of modernity with its stubborn individualism—an individualism that denies the fact that men and women are everywhere found embedded in society in a way that is altogether distinct from citizenship. And this sentiment expressed by Emerson—or any number of modern thinkers—would furthermore be inconceivable in an earlier time. So Locke is undoubtedly still with us, if not in the everyday philosophical expression, at least in our institutions and in our sense of the nature of community life.

---

32. Emerson, *Self-Reliance*, 13.

Safeguarding a Truly Catholic Vision of the World

2. Autonomous Reason

What was different about the Enlightenment sense of reason? When we use the term "autonomous reason" to describe the modern era's peculiar idea of the rational process, we do not imply, of course, that they calculated that reason starts from nothing and operates on its own. Reason is a secondary activity; it must have something furnished to the mind first, then reason responds to what is given. In that sense, the Enlightenment view of reason, which is to say the modem view of reason, is no different from that of the medieval Schoolmen, or from that of the ancients. What is different is both *what* is furnished to the mind and *how* one comes by it—the nature and source of the raw material to which reason responds. For medieval Christian thought, the "given" consists of the three things—revelation, sense experience, and tradition—that connect the human being to the world. These relate the thinking human being to what is present (experience), what is past (tradition), and what is the meaning of things, or one could say the eschatological aim of things.

As matters developed in the Enlightenment era, the material to which reason responds is one of two things. For Descartes and his followers, the firm ground of reason began with an awareness of the distinction between the self and the world, and the awareness of this begins with the narrow point of self-awareness: "I think, therefore I am." All else can be doubted, but the world will be reconstructed rationally from this meager point of reference. That was the approach of the Rationalists.

The Empiricists (notably from Britain, but not all) resembled, in their approach, the Aristotelian. They assumed all knowledge enters the mind through the senses. There is no innate knowledge (Locke), and we are capable of calculations based upon efficient cause and material cause alone, not formal cause or final cause (Hobbes). This is hardly an adequate explanation of either rationalism or empiricism, but it is enough to suggest what these two have in common and what distinguished both of them from earlier philosophies.

What distinguishes the earlier and the later philosophies is also what distinguishes the modern period from all preceding history. The Cartesian philosophy and the Lockean, as examples, depended fundamentally upon that experience which is available to all human beings everywhere. Everyone thinks, and with that they experience the same us Descartes. Everyone absorbs the data of their senses just as Hobbes and Locke do. Everyone does not become a philosopher, of course, but theoretically the fundamentals of philosophy are available to everyone on the same terms. Earlier philosophies, to one extent or another, depend upon experiences that are *not* available to everyone, which are in fact available to very few. For Plato, only a few became philosophers, and upon them the rest were dependent for understanding the right order of the soul and of the city. Aristotle was not so hierarchical in his outlook as Plato, but by the sixteenth century, Aristotelian thought had become so authoritative that the effect was a dependence upon a single philosopher, even though he had been interpreted by a cadre of Muslim, Jewish, and Christian scholars. Besides this, from the beginning of Christianity's broad influence upon Western culture, revelation began to be a decisive factor in shaping philosophy. Revelation is nothing other than the idea that truth important enough to determine the ordering of the human soul and human culture becomes known to us through the rare experiences of a very few members of society over a long period of time. It is a tradition, or a custom, of the most refined and rare type. But the implication is clear: because of these few and these rare, the rest of us come closer to understanding the purpose, the nature, and the shape of life. What this earlier view of philosophy, including that influenced by revealed theology, brings to us is the notion that the many depend upon the few. Philosophy and its benefits is understood in terms of community. In Christian theology, the same effect is reflected in the Pauline doctrine of the *charismata*, gifts acquired by a few for the benefit of the many.

The modern empiricists and rationalists did not find their basis in the rare contribution of the few or the historically past, but in the universally accessible experience of thinking and sensing. Philosophy, in this model, does not theoretically depend upon community, for every person has access to the very thing that makes any person a philosopher. Of course, no one expects everyone to be a philosopher, but perhaps the more salient point is that, for the, modern person, the notion came into vogue that for any philosophy to have legitimacy it must only be *founded* on that which is the experience of all. Locke's *Essay on Human Understanding* is introduced by Locke as taking up an issue of interest to a group of gentlemen of his acquaintance—not philosophers, nor specialists of a theoretical sort, but simply men of the world and of general acquaintance with ideas. This stands in marked contrast to the ancient and medieval philosopher who was free to call upon sources that simply *could not* be verified by just anyone.

Leo Strauss emphasized the fact that the medieval Enlightenment (by which he meant the time of the revival of Aristotelian philosophy from

Avicenna to Maimonides to Aquinas, and which he uses as a term of contrast with the *modern* Enlightenment) was marked by its esoteric nature, which is to say a few philosophers would suffice for any community, just as would a few physicians and a few lawyers and a few master builders. Vocations that actually *contribute* to the life of a community are practiced by the few for the benefit of the many. But "the modern Enlightenment was essentially *exoteric*" (emphasis mine). We must take note of the fact that "the modern Enlightenment, as opposed to the medieval, generally publicizes its teachings."[33]

Let us attempt to parse the difference between these two visions of philosophy and of community life. In the first place, the earlier idea of philosophy presupposes and builds upon the existence of community. For the later view, community might be the topic of philosophy, but one hardly understands the community dependent upon the philosopher, nor the philosopher as servant of the community. Each person is *theoretically* his or her own philosopher. Society is an indiscriminate mass as far as much of modern thought is concerned. It is not a community articulated into a body with interdependent members, a community which in fact benefits from the very distinct and varied *charismata*, but a group of individuals equally endowed (if not with talent and wit) at least with the access to the raw stuff by which the community understands itself.

The modern vision, as one can easily see, is one that tends toward an unarticulated citizenship. And that is the same as saying that people are no longer so bothered by those "tender bonds" which Tennessee Williams once thought so inimical to self-realization. Especially as regards those matters of refined thought and sentiment upon which the order of a society depends, it is, so to speak, "every man for himself." Kant's dictum "Have the courage to think for yourself" frees men and women from the ordering and restraining power of custom, tradition, and transcendent law. It also frees them from each other.

The Enlightenment seized the growing confidence in reason (which was the legacy of the medieval Enlightenment from Anselm to Aquinas) and stood it on its head, so that truth was established by reason rather than reason being established by truth. The growing sense of the dignity of the individual, growing out of Christian revelation, was likewise turned into something that it never was; the dignity of the individual, who lived within a community and within a stream of history, was made into the *sovereignty*

---

33. Strauss, *Philosophy and Law I*, 103.

of the individual—a concept that undermined first the community, then tradition, and finally the dignity of the individual itself.

3. What Is Postmodernism?

So, what then is postmodernism, and why should those, such as evangelicals, who find themselves at odds with the fundamentals of modernity also refuse the sirens of postmodernity in the same way, and for the same reasons, that they resist the secularizing precepts of modernism? I will answer by citing what seems to me an unbiased definition, and then make four concluding points, based upon that definition and the preceding discussion. First, the following definition is offered by Charles Jencks:

> Post-Modernism is fundamentally the eclectic mixture of any tradition with that of the immediate past; it is both the continuation of Modernism and its transcendence. Its best works arc characteristically doubley-coded and ironic, making a feature of the wide choice, conflict and discontinuity of traditions, because the heterogeneity most clearly captures our pluralism.[34]

And finally, four concluding statements:

1. Every culture attempts to speak universally. Art, literature, music, language, evoke a wholeness in the world's fragmented appearance and either purpose or equilibrium in the midst of history's apparent uncertainty.

2. No culture succeeds in doing that. Some, however, have succeeded to an astonishing degree. They articulate a world large enough to transcend and include other cultures, replacing visions confined to tribes and language groups with an understanding of the world large enough to include them all in a powerful ecumenical sentiment. Thus was the influence of Confucianism on Chinese culture, of Islam in the time of the Baghdad Caliphate, of Greek philosophy upon the Greco-Roman period, and more than all, of course, Christianity that swept together the disparate strains of Hebrew prophetism, Greek philosophy, drawing upon streams of traditions from Asia, Europe, and Africa, to present the first—and perhaps the only truly—catholic vision of the world.

---

34. Jencks, *What Is Post-Modernism?*, 7.

3. These cultures also suffer fatigue. Rome once stamped its vision of life on cities from Britain to the Indus Valley. By the third century, one could see that the tide of history was flowing in a different direction. The ruins in the very city of Rome give evidence of the fact that no longer was the world being Romanized so much as Rome was being barbarized; Hadrian's tomb is an example: a great mixture of cultures—a pastiche of Teutonic and classic, of the rustic barbarian with the urban Greco-Roman.

4. Post-modernism is not a culture, but the fatigue of culture. It is a *sign* of the end of modernity, and for that reason its critique of modernity is telling. But it is not a new age, nor the sign of a new kind of culture. It despairs of culture. It cannot become a vessel for gospel for it is fundamentally anti-gospel just as all signs of destruction (or deconstruction) and judgment can only serve as a sort of warning, the invocation of an "Icabod," that the glory has departed. For culture both engenders and depends upon life, not decay, and it is there—not in the decadent features of a modern West, but perhaps in the revivals of Africa and Asia—that we shall truly find the gospel at work. And it is there that a full and viable sense of "vocation" will first be found in a vital and life-giving form.

10

The *Real* Old-Time Religion (2004)

PEOPLE IN THE SOUTH who are intuitively attuned to its culture and history suspect that what passes for popular, evangelical religion in the region is not precisely what it has been in the past.[1] Besides the fact that the South, like other parts of the country, is slowly giving in to the forces of secularism, those states from Maryland to Texas, and halfway up the Mississippi Valley, exhibit a kind of religion that is less distinguishable now, than earlier in their history, from New York, Minnesota, and California. The Crystal Cathedral in Anaheim, California, might just as well be in Atlanta. And the seeker-sensitive Willow Creek Community Church will find its imitators in Oklahoma City, Dallas, and New Orleans. The fundamentalist-liberal rift that once plagued Northern mainline Protestantism, now has its mirror image all across the South, especially in the Southern Baptist Convention.

What the Traditional South Resisted

In order to understand what has changed in the South, it is necessary to have clearly in view the kinds of disorders that the religious communities of the South, whether consciously and intentionally or unconsciously and intuitively, resisted. What they rejected at almost every significant point were three movements that had considerable impact in other parts of the country, and especially in the Northeast. These were (1) fundamentalism, (2) Puritanism, and (3) vulgar pantheism. All three of these have enjoyed

---

1. Originally published in *Southern Partisan* 23, no. 3 (2004): 16–20, 26.

some success in the United States, but until recently none of them have been favorably received in the South. That is not to say that they did not exist in the South: for each represents a kind of permanent temptation for all people everywhere. But each of them also represents something to which some cultures have developed a degree of resistance. The South has historically been somewhat resistant to the first, more resistant to the second, and until relatively recently almost untouched by the third.

The first category will come as a surprise to many: fundamentalism. Often, it is assumed that since the South has been traditionally and so thoroughly influenced by religion, and by a biblical or even biblicist orientation toward religion, there is nowhere that fundamentalism is more at home than in the South. It is not, of course, unknown anywhere. The fundamentalist phenomenon is so frequently found among people of all kinds, and especially those who are less inclined toward non-literal use of language—those who have less of a poetic and metaphorical grasp of reality—that it is descriptive of a certain portion of any population. St. Augustine commented upon this habit among "simple people" in his own day, and never has there been a time without those who think in simple and direct, or literal, categories.

The Church, however, has traditionally understood its teaching as rooted in the historical and literal, but not confined to it. And the South, as it has been represented in the leaders of her churches, has successfully resisted an extreme preoccupation with the mere "facts" of the Bible, and instead saw in these facts a more comprehensive truth. It was, after all, in the North and the Midwest, not the South, that major denominations were split asunder by the fundamentalist-liberal controversy in the 1920s. In the South, inroads were made but were typically marginalized. In North Carolina, William Poteat, president of Wake Forest College wrote favorably of evolution at a time when his Northern peers in denominational colleges would not have dared such; and at home it was little commented upon. B. H. Carroll (1843–1914), theologian and founder of Southwestern Baptist Seminary spoke of Scripture in a way that was distinctly nonfundamentalist. His biographer, Jeff D. Ray, wrote in 1927, at the height of the liberal-fundamentalist controversies in the North, that Carroll,

> believed all the Bible to be true in all that it taught, but his mind was too keenly discriminating to allow him to be trapped by any modern so-called Fundamentalist into saying that it is all literal. He was orthodox, and what might be called an ultra-conservative

The Real Old-Time Religion (2004)

on the plenary and even the verbal inspiration of the Scriptures, but he never felt the necessity of bolstering his orthodoxy by denying that the Bible often teaches deep spiritual truth by means of figurative language.

He found in the Bible something more positive and life-affirming than the fundamentalists knew. After an exceedingly cruel war, in which he lost everything, he searched modern philosophies in a quest for life's meaning. Then, like many young soldiers returning to a devastated homeland, he turned to Christianity. "Once more I viewed the anti-Christian philosophies," he wrote, "no longer to admire them in what they destroyed, but to inquire what they built up, what they offered to a hungry heart and a blasted life." These anti-Christian philosophies were "mere negations," and whoever "looks trustingly into any of its false faces looks into the face of a Medusa, and is turned to stone." In the midst of this search "two books of the Bible took hold of me with unearthly power." They were Job and Ecclesiastes.

There is something rather subtle, but extremely important, in the tone and emphasis that we find in Carroll's reference to the Bible. For Protestants of the South in general, and for B. H. Carroll as a good representative of this sentiment, the Bible was not just an accurate book that could be used to good effect by moralists and religious fanatics, but it was a powerful book, capable of changing lives and forming the human soul.

James Boyce, the Charlestonian founder of the Southern Baptist Theological Seminary in the years before the War Between the States, clarified his doctrine of the Scripture in his massive *Abstract of Systematic Theology*, without so much as alluding to any controversy surrounding their literal or non-literal interpretation. The great Northern theologian A. H. Strong, from a somewhat later period, felt the need to spend more than a hundred pages dealing with just such misunderstandings. The contrast clearly indicates that in the South, as opposed to the North, refinements of expression regarding how Scripture was authoritative had not become a major issue.

The Southern Presbyterian theologians, R. L. Dabney and James Henley Thornwell, spent much time defending the authority of the Bible and the reality of miracles, but not even a paragraph on the literal interpretation of a Scripture that they both saw as pointing not simply to the facts, but through the facts to a transcendent reality. There was plenty of controversy in the South, but it rarely had to do with a strained and factual interpretation of Scripture. There was controversy over ecclesiology (the doctrine of the church) and soteriology (the doctrine of salvation) and Southern theologians had their share of debate, along with the rest of Western Christendom, over divine sovereignty and human free will. But there was evidently little dissatisfaction with a less-than-literal reading of the Bible. For Southerners, there was still no problem in believing that truth is conveyed by poetry, parable, and rhetoric, as well as by straight, hard data. Texas witnessed the great Baptist controversy involving the fundamentalist J. Frank Norris, but his efforts were marginalized, and the juggernaut of the Southern Baptist Convention was not troubled by the spirit of fundamentalism for another sixty years. Today, in the controversy that has troubled these Baptists, the split might be more fairly represented as between the moderates and the conservatives. However, there is plenty of evidence of true fundamentalists playing a part on both sides.

Why only recently has fundamentalism played a significant part in the religion of the South? The most important point is that "fundamentalism," for all its protests against modern ways is actually a modern way of thinking. It has much to do with what Richard Weaver saw as the turning point of Western history: the triumph of nominalism over realism.

For the nominalist, only individual things exist, and what we call universals or principles are only names. This contrasts with the doctrine of St. Thomas—beloved by Southern thinkers from James Petigru Boyce (the Baptist theologian) to Flannery O'Conner (the Catholic writer)—who said that things exist, in the first place, because God creatively thought them. These two contrasting ideas provide for two ways of treating facts. One says that truth or reality lies in the facts themselves. The other holds that facts point beyond themselves to a deeper truth. The former option is nominalism: and it is only under the spell of nominalism that fundamentalism has any appeal. Fundamentalism, therefore, is not an old-fashioned way of thinking, as some assume. The South resisted modernity longer than other parts of the country, and this modernity included fundamentalism.

Fundamentalism, Puritanism and Vulgar Pantheism

The term "fundamentalism" is almost always used in a pejorative sense, and yet I think seldom carefully defined. Often the speaker means religious fanaticism of the sort that might better be called "Puritanism." In the case of Shiite Islam in Iran, and in the case of the Taliban in Afghanistan, the disorder is definitely Puritan, not fundamentalist, though these are often identified as "fundamentalist Islamic" sects or movements. The Puritan wishes to cure the world's ambiguity. He thinks that doing right is a simple matter, to be accomplished with force if necessary. He speaks casually of "solving problems" in society, as if such a thing had ever occurred—as if history had ever yielded anything but slow and uncertain improvements, within enclaves of humane communities, and sometimes within civilizations that stretch over much of a continent. The Puritan neglects mystery and underestimates the depth of sin, even his own. He fails to see that where improvements were made, they were at best ambivalent and desultory. At such times were wonderful glimpses of freedom, goodness, generosity, industry, charity and the like. But never were problems erased as the Puritans of Old England and New England had anticipated. And the ethic of the Puritan brought at least as much disorder as it did improvement.

Fundamentalism is also a disorder, but different from Puritanism. One might say—overstating the case only slightly—that Fundamentalism is a disorder of the intellect, while Puritanism is a disorder of the heart. One, Puritanism, fails to understand the subtlety of the affections, and the elusiveness of the good and the just, both in society and in private lives. Its perfect image is in the scientist of Hawthorne's story "The Birth Mark" who wishes to rid his wife of the one small flaw detracting from her otherwise perfect features, and he ends in taking her life. She is poisoned by the elixir he had prepared for the perfection of her beauty. The other, Fundamentalism, fails to appreciate the subtlety of the intellect, thinking that truth presents itself in univocal and transparent ways to a mind innocent of paradox or metaphor. Its image is Silas Marner, the miser whose understanding of life has been reduced to a commodity that can be seen, and felt, as well as weighed and counted. The symbols of reality have become reality for the fundamentalist.

In Puritanism one often finds an extreme form of Calvinism that would have been foreign to John Calvin himself. Where the goodness of creation is forgotten, the ultimate hope becomes not so much the good news of God rescuing his world from bondage; it becomes instead the triumph of a sovereign God over a fallen world utterly dispossessed of its original goodness. It is a theologizing that has the feel of gnostic speculation. The more contemptuous its doctrine is of experience and the less given to moderation, the more it must be trusted. Nathaniel Hawthorne had complained of the type who, in such a manner, turn moral abstraction into an idol:

Safeguarding a Truly Catholic Vision of the World

> They have no heart, no sympathy, no reason, no conscience. They will keep no friend, unless he make himself the mirror of their purpose; they will smite and slay you, and trample your dead corpse under foot, all the more readily, if you take the first step with them, and cannot take the second, and the third, and every other step of their terribly straight path.

This metaphysical dualism either leaves the world without a God, such as one finds in the deism of the long-forgotten and finally-irrelevant Creator; or else the Deity returns, as in New England Puritanism, striking poor sinners with the rod of moral conquest. The deist God is missing and nature becomes sterile and rational, bereft of warmth or life. It is a disenchanted nature. The Puritan God rules over a nature equally disenchanted, but which is not only alienated from God, but will always pay the price for its alienation.

The Puritan God draws near, in other words, in order to conquer. The love of this God consists of hope on the other side of a mountain of wrath. And while he is near-at-hand (unlike the deist deity), he is morally transcendent, the appalling visitation of absolute justice. In the name of such a God, ethics becomes a weapon with which to subdue nature. And nature becomes the enemy.

Transcendentalism is another religious note that met with timely resistance from Southern theologians such as R. L. Dabney and James Henley Thornwell. It is instructive that Transcendentalism grew up as a prominent successor to Puritanism in a Puritan world. On the surface, this New England philosophy, with its strains of Romanticism and Pantheism, appears to be a reaction against the Puritan metaphysical dualism.

In fact, however, it would seem that the two systems are actually very close. That is, the Puritan's vision of an all-conquering deity is monist (one form of which is pantheism) at heart. This God has no dialogue with his creation; he allows no Sabbath in which his creation can exist on its own; he does not live so much in relationship with the world, and it is difficult to say that such a God loves the world. He can only be understood as existing in sovereign power over it. The reality of the world, with its variety and its differentiation, its separateness, and its independence fades away, as the sovereign reality of a supreme Will becomes the only true thing.

When conquest is complete, the give and take of separate wills, the dialogue of real persons, or of the personality with nature, no longer has any meaning. Only one will counts; and therefore only one will exists. It is difficult to call that will "personal" since personality implies relationship. The Supreme Power relativizes and eventually absorbs all smaller powers—and the radical transcendence of the Puritan deity—Kerboom!—has collapsed the world into itself with the result that what appeared to be a stern dualism turns out to be pantheism. Old John Calvin becomes a whirling dervish in this picture—which is far from historical except in the sense that Cotton Mather, the witch-hunting Calvinist, and his tribe begat Walt Whitman and his own kind of Whirling Dervish—whirling until the world and God, that is, he and God, became one:

> Divine am I inside and out,
> and I make holy whatever I
> touch or am touched from;
> The scent of these arm-pits is
> aroma finer than prayer,
> This head is more than churches or bibles or creeds.
> –"*Song of Myself,*" Stanza 24

The absolute sovereign deity of the Puritan becomes the Unitarian's wedge against the untidy Trinitarian, and finally devolves to the absolute "I" of Whitman's vulgar romanticism.

The South's Incarnational Religion

Between these two—the abstracted Puritan moral principle and the Romantic Pantheism of the Emerson-Thoreau-Whitman variety—lies what I am calling an incarnational sentiment in religion. This describes the most essential character of religion in the American South. A theology that tends to remember, along with its hope for salvation, that the world was created good, and that God became flesh, is not likely to err in the fashion of the ancient Gnostics. That is, it is not likely to promote a hatred of the world and an excessive distrust of humanity. Its doctrine of a fallen humanity does not lead to revolutionary hopes for an alternate world. On the one side, Calvinism has, in its most extreme form, so distanced God from the world that what remains is a yawning chasm between the world and its God. The sense almost inevitably becomes that of an antagonistic dualism, with mind on one side and nature on the other, splitting apart soul and body, reason and passion, word and flesh. The intellect stands to nature as its conqueror. The same sentiment transferred to the exact sciences follows

Safeguarding a Truly Catholic Vision of the World

Descartes's idea that science is intended to make us the "masters and possessors of nature."

Southern religion has always been dominated by a strain of theology that had a healthy respect for nature and the human senses. The Reformed theology of the South, rather than taking on the Gnostic inclination of the New England Puritans and their Unitarian successors, was the sort of Reformed thought influenced heavily by Scottish Common Sense Realism. This, in turn, kept Reformed thought from losing its original respect for natural theology—that is, the idea that we can know something of God through nature, Scripture acting rather as a pair of spectacles by which we might discern God's glory in his created order.

The natural theology of St. Thomas Aquinas still has a bearing upon this branch of Reformed thought. The Baptists and the Methodists, who have made up the largest segment of Southern religion for more than two centuries, are denominations classically shaped by a strong infusion of natural theology. Among the Baptists this was manifested in the degree of reliance on human will and judgment, or "soul competency," as well as by the high degree of localism in their church polity. Among the Methodists, the Arminian theology, with its emphasis upon the human will as it plays a part in the divine economy, bears within it a certain resistance to a one-sided view of divine power. The Presbyterians and Episcopalians who have, since the early nineteenth century, influenced Southern thought to a degree outweighing their numbers, also strongly reflect this positive view of nature, creation, and the incarnation. The Roman Catholics, who even in the nineteenth century accounted for much of the population in the regions of the old Louisiana territory, naturally reflect the interplay of natural and revealed theology that has long been a hallmark of Catholic thought.

The strong development of a natural theology in the West can be attributed to two main influences. One is the great theological synthesis of St. Thomas Aquinas; and the other is Reformed thought following in the tradition of John Calvin. It is interesting that, when James Petigru Boyce, the founding president of the Southern Baptist Theological Seminary, taught theology to his upper level, Latin-reading students, he concentrated upon two major thinkers: Francis Turrettin, the Calvinist systematic theologian, and Thomas Aquinas.

The Real *Old-Time Religion (2004)*

Southern Religion and the Lost Cause

It is worth mentioning that the very fact of the South's brutal experience of war, and its humiliating defeat, played a part in that section's resistance of a religious error that has otherwise seemed endemic to the United States. It is the same error to which ancient Israel was so prone: the belief that right religion would always triumph, and defeat is a sign of divine disfavor. This error belongs to the adolescence of religion, but not to its maturity, as the prophets Jeremiah, and Ezekiel, were to teach their people. Southerners also had to deal with their own defeat and ruin, as well as with the eventual recognition of their own sins—even while the virtues of their oppressors were exaggerated and their sins ignored.

Nevertheless, certain virtues can only come prominently into play under conditions that are mostly foreign to the bourgeois comforts of twentieth-century America. Flannery O'Conner worried that Southerners were losing this sense of difference and alienation that has something in common with the very idea of holiness. She said once, "The Anguish that most of us have observed for some time now has been caused not by the fact that the South is alienated from the rest of the country, but by the fact that it is not alienated enough, that everyday we are getting more and more like the rest of the country, that we are being forced out, not only of our many sins but of our few virtues."

Conclusion
Bradley G. Green

I AM THANKFUL THAT Jacob Shatzer has chosen to take the time and effort to collect these essays by A. J. Conyers. While most of us in the academy desire to get our ideas published in book form, it is hard to improve upon a well-written essay. And Conyers wrote many such essays. In this collection readers can see the breadth of Conyers's interests, reading, and expertise. One can also see—and I will return to this—that Conyers was something of a unique voice in Baptist theology.

I want to do a few brief things in this conclusion. First, I want to draw attention to the breadth and variety of Conyers's scholarship as featured in these essays. Second, I want to share something of what Chip Conyers meant to me. Third, I want to suggest why Chip Conyers was in fact a unique voice in Baptist theology.

The Variety of A. J. Conyers's Interests

First, I draw attention to the breadth and variety of Conyers's interests. Conyers had a wide array of interests. As the essays in this book demonstrate, Conyers's interests ranged from the theology of Jürgen Moltmann—whom Conyers both appreciated, but to whose theology he mounted a significant challenge, to the nature of theology in light of the Holocaust, to the place of the liberal arts, to the southern intellectual tradition—including southern writers like William Gilmore Simms as well as the nature of "southern religion," to the nature of post-conservative and/or postmodern approaches to theology, to the importance of the liberal arts, to a Christian understanding of the Enlightenment and modernity, to the nature of what is unique or central to being a Baptist, to the relationship between Protestant and Catholic theology, and much more.

While these loci might seem varied (and they are), there is nonetheless a fundamental unity. At the most basic level, Conyers was a theologian—and hence all things were fair game for intellectual deliberation and consideration. We should also say that Conyers was a "traditional" theologian in that he valued—and affirmed—the insights of the historic Christian tradition, and was wary of trendy fads. Conyers was willing to both affirm the importance and centrality of 2,000 years of Christian thought while nonetheless being willing to work out his own particular theological construals as he deemed appropriate. Thus, while seeing great value in the broader catholic tradition, Conyers remained a Protestant—indeed a Baptist—until his death.

But more pointedly, one sees a unity in Conyers's essays if one realizes that he was interested in the importance of the theological task in light of the where he found himself—theologizing amidst the ruins of late modernity. Given where he found himself, Conyers found insight in an older conservatism (especially thinkers like Richard Weaver), and in the southern intellectual tradition (hence his interest in the novelist and poet William Gilmore Simms, as well as more recent thinkers like Donald Livingston).

While some Protestants who find themselves drinking deeply from the wells of the patristic and medieval theologians end up heading to Rome or to Eastern Orthodoxy, Conyers drank from such wells while still affirming his Baptist convictions. Indeed, Conyers was unconvinced that the Baptist movement was simply one more manifestation of modernity. Rather, under God's mysterious providence, Baptists—at their best, (1) were in fundamental continuity with the catholic tradition of which it was a part, and (2) advanced needed and proper insights which were ultimately necessary if the church was truly going to be reformed according to Holy Writ.

A. J. Conyers as Mentor

One of the highlights of my doctoral program (at Baylor University) was my relationship with A. J. Conyers. It was an interesting time to be at Baylor, and my relationship with him was something of a lifeline for me. I started the PhD program at Baylor in 1994, the same year that George W. Truett Theological Seminary (Baylor University) was just starting. Conyers came from South Carolina to serve as one of the founding faculty members at Truett, teaching theology. In Truett's early days, its promotional literature emphasized that it was going to be both Evangelical and Baptist. This was a perfect fit for Conyers. I met Chip about a year into my doctoral program.

During one of our early conversations, I asked Chip about those thinkers who had influenced him most. When he began to speak of Richard Weaver and Eric Voegelin and Gerhart Niemeyer, I knew that Chip was someone I wanted to get to know better. Chip had cancer, and I would eventually end up teaching his courses for him at Truett, during the spring of 1998. Chip was receiving treatment, but recovered enough that he returned to the classroom during that spring, and he and I would team-teach his courses for the last part of the spring.

As I grappled with choosing a research topic for my dissertation, I spent some time reading Jacques Derrida, thinking I might try to write on this key figure. Subtly and tactfully, Chip suggested that I might actually want to write on something more explicitly theological. I eventually followed his advice. My topic—a study in the theology of Colin Gunton in light of Augustine—very much bears the mark of Conyers's influence. Like Conyers himself, Gunton was concerned with offering a theological account and critique of modernity. This topic allowed me to explore many of the interests and concerns that Conyers and I shared: how to think theologically amidst late modernity, *and* how to think theologically *about* the nature of modernity itself. The dissertation process allowed Conyers and me to continue to correspond and think together about issues Conyers always maintained an interest in, and issues which continue to animate my own thinking as well. He was a Doctor Father in the best sense.

A. J. Conyers as a Unique Voice in Baptist Theology

To understand the uniqueness of A. J. Conyers, one has to have at least a little understanding of the state of Baptist life in the 80s, 90s, and 2000s. The Southern Baptist Convention since 1979 had been in turmoil, with "Conservatives" or "Fundamentalists" engaging in a "resurgence" or "takeover" from the "Moderates" or "Liberals" (the viability of these terms all depend on how one views this crucial phase of SBC life). Conyers had never been a partisan on behalf of the Conservatives or the Moderates. He was a member of the Evangelical Theological Society (where membership includes an affirmation of biblical inerrancy), and was certainly a Baptist and traditional

Protestant—although a Protestant with a great love and appreciation for the Catholic tradition. Conyers had no interest in the liberalism which sometimes pervades Moderate Baptist circles, but he was not simply an activist within the Conservative movement or cause within the SBC.

It is against such a backdrop that one has to read and understand Conyers's essay in this book, "The Changing Face of Baptist Theology" (originally appearing in 1998). Conyers here engages in both an analysis of the contemporary Baptist scene, and towards the end of the essay really hits his stride—offering an incisive critique of the viability of post-conservatism and postmodernism. But Conyers does not pose as someone who is "above the fray." Rather, he just wrote good theology. As C. S. Lewis suggested toward the end of *Mere Christianity*, the Christian's duty is simply to tell the truth as best as he can. The goal is not to be *original*. Rather, if one simply tells the truth, one will end up telling the truth *and*—more often than not—will be strikingly original.

In light of all this, this set of essays is important in introducing readers to one of the finest Baptist theologians of his day. The difficulty of being a Baptist in a post-SBC controversy world, is that there is a certain pressure to toe this or that line. If one has more sympathy with the Conservatives, there are both formal and informal lines one should not cross. If one has more sympathy with the Moderates, there are likewise both formal and informal lines one should not cross. In reading Conyers, one is reading someone who was not—in a sense—playing that game. He was simply trying to write good theology and, on my view, succeeded.

I am thankful that Jacob Shatzer found A. J. Conyers to be a helpful guide. Conyers was such a guide for me, and through this set of essays, as well as Shatzer's dissertation (and forthcoming book), readers can appreciate the insights of wisdom of a fellow pilgrim, and can likewise walk with a guide who can be of assistance as we sojourn to that city not made with hands.

Bibliography

Abrahams, Israel. "Sabbath (Jewish)." In *Encyclopedia of Religion and Ethics*, vol. 10. Edited by James Hastings. Edinburgh: T & T Clark, 1918.
Alviar, José. *Klesis: The Theology of the Christian Vocation According to Origen*. Dublin, Ireland, 1993.
Aquinas, *Commentary on the Metaphysics of Aristotle*. Translated by John P. Rowan. Chicago: Henry Regnery, 1961.
Arendt, Hannah. *The Origins of Totalitarianism*. New York: Harcourt, Brace, Jovanovich, 1973.
Augustine, *Confessions*. Translated by R. S. Pine-Coffin. London: Penguin, 1961.
Berkovitz, Eliezer. *Faith after the Holocaust*. New York: KTAV Publishing House, 1973.
Bonhoeffer, Dietrich. *Ethics*. New York: Touchstone, 1995.
Burrell, David B. "Convictions and Operative Warrant." In *Theology Without Foundations: Religious Practice and the Future or Theological Truth*, 43–48. Edited by Stanley Hauerwas, Nancey Murphy, and Mark Nation. Nashville: Abingdon, 1994.
Calvin, *Institutes of the Christian Religion*.
Clement of Alexandria, *Stromateis*. Translated by John Ferguson. Washington, D.C.: The Catholic University of America Press, 1991.
Conrads, Ulrich, ed. *Programmes and Manigestoes on Twentieth-Century Architecture*. Translated by Michael Bullock. London: Lund Humphries, 1970.
Conyers, Deborah A., and James C. Conyers. "Biography of A. J. 'Chip' Conyers." In *Thriving in Babylon: Essays in Honor of A. J. Conyers*, edited by David B. Capes and J. Daryl Charles, xi–xxxix. Eugene, OR: Pickwick, 2011.
Derrida, Jacques. *Writing and Difference*. Translated by Alan Bass. Chicago: University of Chicago Press, 1978.
Descartes, René. *Discours de la Methode* (1692). In *Oeuvres Philosophiques* I. Edited by Ferdinande Alquie. Paris: Garnier, 1963.
Dewey, John. *The Quest for Certainty*. New York: Minton, Balch & Company, 1929.
Ellul, Jacques. *The New Demons*. Translated by C. Edward Hopkin. New York: Seabury Press, 1973.
Emerson, Ralph Waldo. *Self-Reliance*. Mount Vernon, NY: Peter Pauper Press, 1967.
Erickson, Millard. *Postmodernising the Faith: Evangelical Responses to the Challenge of Postmodernism*. Grand Rapids, MI: Baker, 1998.
———. *The Evangelical Left*. Grand Rapids: Baker, 1997.

Bibliography

Estep, William R. *The Anabaptist Story.* Nashville: Broadman, 1963.
Farmer, James Oscar Jr. *The Metaphysical Confederacy.* Macon, GA: Mercer University Press, 1986.
Fleisher, Eva, ed. *Auschwitz: Beginning of a New Era?* New York: KTAV Publishing House, 1977.
Forde, Gerhard O. *On Being a Theologian of the Cross: Reflections on Luther's Heidelberg Disputation, 1518.* Grand Rapids, MI: Eerdmans, 1997.
Foster, Frank Hugh. A *Genetic History of the New England Theology.* New York: Russell & Russell, 1963.
Friedrich, Karl J., ed. *The Philosophy of Kant.* New York: The Modern Library, 1993.
Fukuyama, Francis. *The End of History and the Last Man.* New York: Avon Books, 1992.
Garrett, James Leo Jr., E. Glenn Hinson, and James E. Tull, eds. *Are Southern Baptists Evangelicals?* Macon, GA: Mercer University Press, 1983.
George, Timothy. "Review of Thomas J. Nettles, *By His Grace and for His Glory.*" *Review & Expositor* 84 (Winter 1987): 142–44.
———. "The Reformed Doctrine of Believers' Baptism." *Interpretation* 47 (July 1993): 242–54.
———. *Theology of the Reformers.* Nashville: Broadman, 1988.
Grenz, Stanley J. *A Primer on Postmodernism.* Grand Rapids: Eerdmans, 1996.
———. and John R. Franke, *Beyond Foundationalism: Shaping Theology in a Postmodern Context.* Louisville, KY: Westminster John Knox Press, 2001.
———, *Revisioning Evangelical Theology.* Downers Grove, Illinois: InterVarsity Press, 1993.
Hauerwas, Stanley, Nancey Murphy, and Mark Nation, eds. *Theology Without Foundations: Religious Practice and the Future or Theological Truth.* Nashville: Abingdon, 1994.
Heschel, A. J. *The Sabbath, Its Meaning for Modern Man.* New York: Farrar, Strauss, 1952.
Hilary of Poitiers, *The Trinity.* New York: Fathers of the Church, Inc., 1954.
Jencks, Charles. *What Is Post-Modernism?* 3rd ed. New York, NY: St. Martin's Press, 1989.
Kafka, Franz. *Parables and Paradoxes.* New York, 1958.
Kirk, G. S. and J. E. Raven, *The Presocratic Philosophies.* New York: Cambridge University Press, 1971.
Kraus C. J., "Über den Pantheismus," *Vermischte Schriften.*
Lassman, Peter, Irving Velody, and Herminio Martins, eds., *Max Weber's 'Science as a Vocation.'* London: Unwin Hyman, 1989.
Luther, *Luther's Works.* Philadelphia: Concordia.
Marcuse, Herbert. *Negations.* Boston: Beacon Press, 1968.
Marty, Martin. "Baptistification Takes Over." *Christianity Today* 27 no. 13 (September 2, 1983), 33–36.
McBeth, Leon. *The Baptist Heritage.* Nashville: Broadman, 1987.
McClendon, James and James M. Smith, *Understanding Religious Convictions.* Notre Dame, IN: University of Notre Dame Press.
McClendon, James. *Ethics: Systematic Theology,* vol. 1. Nashville: Abingdon, 1986.
Mead, Sydney Earl. *Nathaniel William Taylor, 1786–1858: A Connecticut Liberal.* Chicago: University of Chicago Press, 1942.
Mohler, Jr., R. Albert. "The Eclipse of God at Century's End: Evangelicals Attempt Theology without Theism." *The Southern Baptist Journal of Theology* 1 (Spring 1997): 6–15.

Moltmann, Jürgen. *God in Creation.* Translated by Margaret Kohl. San Francisco: Harper, 1985.

———. *The Church in the Power of the Spirit.* Translated by Margaret Kohl. New York: Harper & Row, 1977.

———. *The Crucified God.* Translated by R. A. Wilson and John Bowden. London: SCM, 1974.

———. *The Experiment Hope.* Edited and translated by Douglas Meeks. Philadelphia: Fortress Press, 1975.

Murphy, Nancey. "Introduction." In *Theology Without Foundations: Religious Practice and the Future or Theological Truth*, 9–31. Edited by Stanley Hauerwas, Nancey Murphy, and Mark Nation. Nashville: Abingdon, 1994.

Nettles, Thomas J. *By His Grace and for His Glory: A Historical, Theological, and Practical Study of the Doctrines of Grace in Baptist Life.* Grand Rapids, MI: Baker, 1986.

Niemeyer, Gerhart. *Between Nothingness and Paradise.* Baton Rouge: Louisiana State University Press, 1971.

———. *Within and Above Ourselves: Essays in Political Analysis.* Wilmington, DE: 1996.

Pattison, Robert. *The Triumph of Vulgarity.* New York: Oxford University, 1987.

Pieper, Josef. *"Divine Madness": Plato's Case against Secular Humanism.* Translated by Lothar Krauth. San Francisco: Ignatius, 1995.

———. *The Silence of St. Thomas.* Translated by John Murray, S.J., and Daniel O'Connor. South Bend, IN: St. Augustine Press, 1999.

Rorty, Richard. *The Consequences of Pragmatism.* Minneapolis: University of Minnesota Press, 1982.

Rosenzweig, Franz. *The Star of Redemption.* Translated by William W. Hallo. Boston: Beacon Press, 1972.

Rubenstein, Richard L. *After Auschwitz: Radical Theology and Contemporary Judaism.* Indianapolis: Bobbs-Merril, 1966.

———. *The Cunning of History: The Holocaust and the American Future.* New York: Harper & Row, 1978.

Simms, William Gilmore. *Sabbath Lyrics.* Charleston, SC: The Press of Walker and James, 1849.

———. *Self-Development.* Milledgeville, GA: Thalian Society, 1847.

———. *The Social Principle.* Tuscaloosa, AL: The Eropsophic Society of the University of Alabama, 1843.

Southern, R. W. *Western Society and the Church in the Middle Ages.* London: Penguin, 1970.

Spragens, Jr., Thomas A. *The Politics of Motion: The World of Thomas Hobbes.* Lexington, KY: University Press of Kentucky, 1973.

Stassen, Glen. "Anabaptist Influences in the Origin of the Particular Baptists," *Mennonite Quarterly Review 36* (October 1962): 322–48.

Strauss, Leo. *Philosophy and Law I.* Albany, NY: SUNY Press, 1995.

Tate, Allen. *Essays of Four Decades.* Chicago: Swallow, 1968.

Thielicke, Helmut. *Between Heaven and Earth.* Translated by John Doberstein. New York: Harper & Row, 1965.

———. *Theological Ethics*, vol. 1: *Foundations.* Edited by William H. Lazareth. Philadelphia: Fortress Press, 1966.

Bibliography

Tull, James. "'Evangelicals' and Baptists—The Shape of the Question." In *Are Southern Baptists Evangelicals?*, 1–30. Edited by James Leo Garrett Jr., E. Glenn Hinson, and James E. Tull. Macon, GA: Mercer University Press, 1983.

Voegelin, Eric. *Revolution and the New Science*. Vol. 6 of *History of Political Ideas*. Vol. 24 of *The Collected Works of Eric Voegelin*. Columbia, MO: University of Missouri Press, 1998.

Weaver, Richard. *Ideas Have Consequences*. Chicago: University of Chicago.

White, Barrington Raymond. *The English Baptists of the Seventeenth Century*. London: The Baptist Historical Society, 1983.

———. *The English Separatist Tradition*. New York: Oxford University Press, 1971.

Wiesel, Elie. *Night*. Translated by Stella Rodway. New York: Hill & Wang, 1960.

Yates, Frances A. *Giordano Bruno and the Hermetic Tradition*. New York: Vintage, 1969.

www.ingramcontent.com/pod-product-compliance
Lightning Source LLC
Chambersburg PA
CBHW050831160426
43192CB00010B/1984